The Book of Numbers

31st January 2021 – lulu - global

A4 LULU

First Printing: [2020,2021]

ISBN <978-1-716-16375-3 >

adrianbonni@gmx.com

Our body is just the universe in miniature and one who understands Heretics would note the significance of this – AS ABOVE SO BELOW.

Subjects covered in this book:-

2

INTRODUCTION

"Just look at us. Everything is backwards, everything is upside down. Doctors destroy health, lawyers destroy justice, psychiatrists destroy minds, scientists destroy truth, major media destroys information, religions destroy spirituality and governments destroy freedom."
— Michael Ellner

I originally did this book in A5 format, but proof copy had errors mainly in drawings. So now redone in A4.

I have then added information on Washington DC, Stonehenge and the Pyramids of Egypt and how they are related.

The method schools use to teach young children basic mathematics is called rope learning. They get them to chant 1 x 2 = 2; 2 x 2 = 4; 3 x 2 = 6 for example. This may give knowledge but it does not give understanding. Understanding in life often comes from doing something wrong, realising you made an error. Then doing the thing again but without the error to get the correct result. By cross referencing you can get to the correct result. If someone wants to know what 9 x 9 is – then it is better to do 9 x 10 and takeaway 9.

If you asked anyone who has left school what the numbers 1 – 100 add up to most won't be able to answer. Yet someone who thinks inside the box using the brain they have been born with will see there are 50 pairs of 101's so the answer is 50 x 101 or 5050.

It is same with Doctors you go to see them with high blood pressure. They then give you a tablet to lower your blood pressure. This pill lowers your blood pressure but also reduces oxygen to vital areas of the brain like the Hippocampus resulting in age related illness years later. They cure one thing to give you another thing. [See my book on healing using sound frequencies.]

We have some who just accept what society tells them. They just accept there was a big bang – see my book on "Everything you think you know is a lie". Schools won't allow people to challenge these basic ideas like Darwin which have no proof in evidence.

Many just accept Gravity as fact yet have not had the idea or intellect to think about other possibilities. All children are born Gnostics asking what does this do and why? But the system destroys this. We should all be seekers of the truth. There is so much fake news and ideas at the moment that we must cross reference many times and then go with our gut instinct. You should never think just one religion has all the answers.

If there is evidence of a consciousness that created our universe I believe it can be found in Nature and Physics. Everything in the Universe is Electro-magnetic waveforms. We can observe the Golden Ratio in plants and measurements of our own body parts. The universal language is mathematics. I also think that just like DNA is coded then language is also encoded as it comes from the source also must follow strict rules and knowing the origin of words can help us understand our true purpose our PLAN on the Planet.

Unfortunately our planet is now under control of the illuminati and other secret societies hell bent on destroying man from his true divinity.

Some pages in the book deal with the secret societies and give proof that the conspiracy is real. Conspiracy means Spiro [to breath] and Con [together]. This is why they take blood oaths not to reveal their secrets with the normal people of this world.

The 12 x 5 Maths given to us from the Sumerians

The Sumerians say they were given their 12 x 5 system of maths from the Anunnaki which translates as those who from the sky came.

We get the 12 from the 4 fingers of the Left hand and the 3 division on each finger.

We get the 5 from the digits on the right hand – the 4 fingers plus the thumb.

Time is 1 second. We have 60 in a minute (12 x 5)

All geometry is based on base 60 and is probably the key to understanding the Universe. Pythagoras found all music notes using the system of 5th's and if you half the length of a string then its pitch doubles or the frequency is double. Before joining the Pythagoras school you had to keep a vow of silence for 5 years. This school was burnt down and most members were killed so little is known of their knowledge. The same happened to the Library of Alexandra – this was burned down but was some books looted before this event? Does Vatican have this old knowledge? Alexandria used to copy any document found on a ship at their ports including maps and knowledge and put them in the great library.

Most ancient instruments vibrate at 432 Hertz. The Rockefellers got this music tuning changed to 440 Hertz.

Pythagoras found the number 432 using maths and not music instruments.

A triangle = 180 degrees.

Circle and Square are both 360.

Pentagon is 540.

[These shapes are called Platonic solids]

Platonic solids can be 2D or 3D.

The numbers all add up to 9.

[See my book on consciousness creates reality to understand the 3, 6, and 9]

There are 2160 days in the Great Year which takes into account the wobble caused by the Earths tilt.

2160 miles is also the diameter of our moon.

2160 /2 = Octagon

2160 / 3 = hexagon

2160 /4 = pentagon

2160 / 5 = 432 (Hertz)

2160 / 6 = 360 (Square / Circle)

216 is half 432

We have 43200 seconds in the day and 43200 in the night.

432 x 432 = speed of light

5 x 12 mathematics gives us the 12 inches in an imperial foot

12 are a dozen.

Using the Formula $F = 1/T$

If we assume the 1 is the biggest number then this is the great year of 25,920

And if we assume time is 1 minute or 60 seconds we then get:-

$F = 25920 / 60$

This then gives us the magic number 432 Hertz

$12 \times 12 = 144$

$= 1440 = 144,000$ etc

We have 144,000 casing stones in the Egyptian Pyramid. 144,000 chosen ones go to heaven in the bible but we must remember that the Bible is a cloak this is just another way of saying the number 9 which is the number of enlightenment based on Vortex Vector maths. The number 9 is the number of the source or the unified field where only stillness exists. This is the root of our origin the original consciousness that from this all everything came. The Bible contains Exoteric and Esoteric knowledge. Only Adepts can see the esoteric knowledge.

There was never a big bang just silence which the Egyptians called Nu

The factor of 9 is the singularity the point in the middle of the ring.

$144,000 / 432 = 333.33$ to infinity

THE FIBONACCI CODE IN EVERYTHING?

There seems to be maths sequence in Nature is this the fingerprint of God? It is 0,1,1,2,3,5,8.

The last number is the sum of the two before it. This pattern can be found in sea shells and our universe. Also the 3, 6, 9 is present the key to the universe.

In mathematics and computing, Fibonacci coding is a universal code which encodes positive integers into binary code words. It is one example of representations of integers based on Fibonacci numbers. Each code word ends with "11" and contains no other instances of "11" before the end.

The Fibonacci code is closely related to the Zeckendorf representation, a positional numeral system that uses Zeckendorf's theorem and has the property that no number has a representation with consecutive 1s. The Fibonacci code word for a particular integer is exactly the integer's Zeckendorf representation with the order of its digits reversed and an additional "1" appended to the end.

1.61803 or Φ (phi) is called Golden ratio and human finger sizes between bones relate to this which is Fibonacci code.

Binary   1.1001111000110111011

Decimal 1.6180339887498948482

Fibonacci   **_BINARY_**

Fibonacci	BINARY
0	0
1	1
1	1
2	10
3	11
5	101
8	1000
13	1101
21	10101

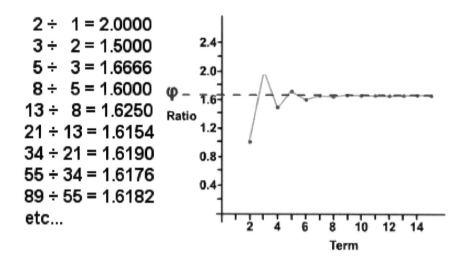

The Golden Ratio φ can be approximated by
a process of successively dividing each term
in the Fibonacci Sequence by the previous term.

With each successive division, the ration comes
closer and closer to a value of 1.618033987...

$2 \div 1 = 2.0000$
$3 \div 2 = 1.5000$
$5 \div 3 = 1.6666$
$8 \div 5 = 1.6000$
$13 \div 8 = 1.6250$
$21 \div 13 = 1.6154$
$34 \div 21 = 1.6190$
$55 \div 34 = 1.6176$
$89 \div 55 = 1.6182$
etc...

When a plant starts growth it is not close to the Golden Ratio. As the plant grows then it will try to get as close to it as possible. I suspect each evolution of man involves taking us down the Golden Ratio to another state of being and this is why missing links not found as new binary codes from Matrix get downloaded when time is right for an upgrade.

NUMBER 40

Of all the types and shadows of the Old Testament, none is as pervasive and important as the shadows revealed in the relationship between "forty," and the fulfilment of promises.

The rains (in Noah's day) fell for 40 days and nights (Genesis 7:4).
Israel ate Manna for 40 years (Exodus 16:35).
Moses was with God in the mount, 40 days and nights (Exodus 24:18).

Moses was again with God 40 days and 40 nights (Exodus 34:28).

Moses led Israel from Egypt at age 80 (2 times 40), and after 40 years in the wilderness, died at 120 (3 times 40; Deuteronomy 34:7).

The spies searched the land of Canaan for 40 days (Numbers 13:25).

Therefore, God made Israel wander for 40 years (Numbers 14:33-34).

40 stripes was the maximum whipping penalty (Deuteronomy 25:3).

God allowed the land to rest for 40 years (Judges 3:11).

God again allowed the land to rest for 40 years (Judges 8:28).

Abdon (a judge in Israel) had 40 sons (Judges 12:14).

Israel did evil; God gave them to an enemy for 40 years (Judges 13:1).

Eli judged Israel for 40 years (1 Samuel 4:18).

Saul reigned for 40 years (Acts 13:21).

Ishbosheth (Saul's son) was 40 when he began reign (2 Samuel 2:10).

David reigned over Israel for 40 years (2 Samuel 5:4, 1 Kings 2:11).

The holy place of the temple was 40 cubits long (1 Kings 6:17).

The sockets of silver are in groups of 40 (Exodus 26:19 & 21).

Solomon reigned same length as his father; 40 years (1 Kings 11:42).

Ezekiel's (symbolic) temple is 40 cubits long (Ezekiel 41:2).

Jesus fasted 40 days and nights (Matthew 4:2).

Jesus was tempted 40 days (Luke 4:2, Mark 1:13).

Jesus remained on earth 40 days after resurrection (Acts 1:3).

Women are pregnant **for 40 weeks** (time of testing).

The number forty is used by God to represent a period of testing or judgment (the length of time necessary to accomplish some major part of Gods plan in his dealings with various portions of mankind). The 40 days of rain in the days of the flood were the judgments of God. The 40 day periods of fasting, testing, and communing with God that were faced by Moses and Jesus were a form of God's judgments. The forty years that the Israelites spent in the wilderness were also the judgments of God. Various leaders in Israel who reigned for 40 year periods were put there BY God according to His Will and Judgments. Egypt was left desolate for 40 years because of God's judgments. I could go on and on, but I think these examples should suffice for now.

The maximum number of "stripes" allowed for punishment was 40. "Stripes" have to do with judgment (including

God's). See Luke 12:47-48. When God brings judgment upon His people, it may be rightly termed, "stripes". When Peter states (about Jesus) "by whose stripes ye were healed" in 1 Peter 2:24, he is quoting from Isaiah 53:5 which is a prophecy concerning spiritual and not physical healing as many teach. Although physical healing from God is a wonderful blessing, spiritual healing is an even greater blessing. Our salvation is dependent on the fact that Jesus bore the stripes that you and I deserve to bear. In other words, Jesus' bore the main force of the judgments that should come upon you and I as sinners. Isaiah's prophecy shows the judgments of God were poured out upon Jesus for our healing.

Forty sons of a judge in Israel (Abdon), whose name means "servitude" represents the product or offspring of a judge who serves in Israel. Once again we see the number 40 used in connection with the subject of judgment.

The Numerological Meaning of 777

Therefore, the number 7 is regarded as the number of hidden, inner wisdom. There is a force in the universe that is giving your life its particular shape.

Our traditions refer to this force in a variety of different ways, including God, spirit or source. 7 refers to our connection with this hidden essence which is founded on creativity and the ability to attract to ourselves the material circumstances that we want by focusing our attention in the right way.

777 is the number 7 three times. When a number is repeated it is as though its essence has been multiplied, in this case

three times, making 777 the number of our inner wisdom becoming focused in creative activity, ultimately finding a foundation in material reality. The Astral plane has 7 planes these all exist in the same space. We have the Physical plane that we exist on. The next is the plane of Forces, the next the Astral, the next the mental plane. The 3 above the mental plane are what Christians would call heaven. Each plane has 7 sub divisions and these have another 7 subdivisions – this gives the 777.

Number 6

$1 \times 2 \times 3 = 6$ but so does $1+2+3$

A cube is 6 and represents **the Body** a Pentagram 5 represents the microcosm.

Number 10

Made from $1+2+3+4$

Where 1 is a point, 2 is a line, 3 is a plane and 4 our 3D reality of plane moving downwards.

Summing up 888

The Angel's numbers are best interpreted by adding the SUM of the numbers, as well as interpreting the individual numbers.

$8+8+8 = 24, \quad 2+4 = 6$

Adding $8+8+8$, you get the sum total of 24, which can be further reduced to the number 6. The numbers 2, 4, 6 and 8 are all activated! Therefore the number 888 contains all our single digit even numbers. The even numbers represent BALANCE between heaven and earth, your heart and mind, the spiritual and material realms, work and play – as well as HARMONY IN RELATIONSHIPS.

When you are truly expressing your divine gifts with confidence, you are in your power, and your relationships improve, as well as your bank account and quality of life.

888 is a repeating digit (a number all of whose digits are equal), and a strobogrammatic number (one that reads the same upside-down on a seven-segment calculator display). 888 x 888 x 888 = 700227072 is the smallest cube in which each digit occurs exactly three times, and the only cube in which three distinct digits each occur three times. 888 the smallest multiple of 24 whose digit sum is 24, and as well as being divisible by its digit sum it is divisible by all of its digits.

888 is a practical number, meaning that every positive integer up to 888 itself may be represented as a sum of distinct divisors of 888.

There are exactly 888 trees with four unlabeled and three labelled nodes, exactly 888 seven-node undirected graphs without isolated vertices,[9] and exactly 888 non-alternating knots whose crossing number is 12.

Symbology and numerology

In Christian numerology, the number 888 represents Jesus, or sometimes more specifically Christ the Redeemer. This representation may be justified either through Gematria, by counting the letter values of the Greek transliteration of Jesus' name, or as an opposing value to 666, the number of the beast

In Chinese numerology, the number 888 has a different meaning, triple fortune, a strengthening of the meaning of the digit 8. For this reason, addresses and phone numbers containing the digit sequence 888 are considered particularly lucky, and may command a premium because of it.

TESLA

Tesla said to understand our universe think in terms of energy, frequency and vibration.

He also said understanding the numbers 3, 6 and 9 unlock the key to our universe. The universe is electro-magnetic and a Torus. The number 9 creates all the other numbers from Vortex maths.

PATENTS IN 1943 RIGHT AFTER TESLA DIED WITH…
U.S. SUPREME COURT DECISION #369.
What are the chances it would be decision # 3 – 6 – 9?
At least one in three hundred and sixty nine. RIGHT?

Nikola Tesla caused the September 1899 Cape Yakataga and Yakutat Bay earthquakes in Alaska from Colorado

Springs.

On...

September 3, 1899 [9, 3, 9]

September 6, 1899 [9, 6, 9]

September 9, 1899 [9, 9, 9]

"If you only knew the magnificence of the three, the six and the nine... then you would have a key to the universe." - Nikola Tesla

(AFTER CAUSING 3 EARTHQUAKES)

ZERO, ONE, TWO, THREE, FOUR, FIVE, SIX, SEVEN, EIGHT and NINE: These ten principles united represent completion, the perfection of all being and the harmony that exists within the demiurgic word of the creator, once again, apparent on the two hands that lay right before you. These ten principles are the living thoughts of a great creator being, a great mystery or grand architect who is within all things and without which, all things would cease to exist.

 MOON = 2,160 Miles (2+1+6= 9)

 SUN = 864,000 Miles (8+6+4=18 & 1+8= 9)

 EARTH = 7,920 Miles (7+9+2=18 & 1+8= 9)

The ancient Vedic peoples, responsible for the oldest of Hindu scriptures, reiterated the supremacy of this base-ten system by placing nine numbers around a circle/zero and performing their math in this way. By placing 9 at the top and moving clockwise around the circle, these 9 digits encased the wholly / holy zero with the zero performing its magic as the placeholder for the rest of the digits.

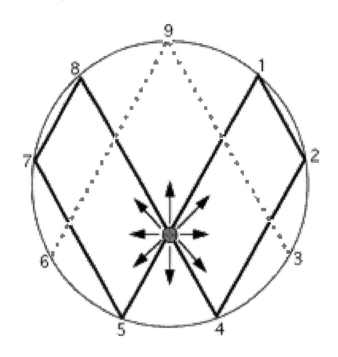

SYMBOL OF ENLIGHTENMENT ABOVE

A number cannot be created or destroyed and zero does not exist on a number line or in any multiplication series.

The number 9 is the node and represents Spirit.

The numbers 3 and 6 represent the Yin and Yang in the form of magnetism and the number 9 is the S curve. The base ten numerical counting system is triangulated.

Infinity has an epicentre.

The powers of ten occur by halving.

20

The torus skin models harmonic cascadence.

Our base-ten decimal system is not manmade; rather it is created by this flow of energy. Amazingly, after twenty years of working with this symbol and collaborating with engineers and scientists, Marko discovered that the 1, 2, 4,8,7,5 was a doubling circuit for a very efficient electrical coil.

There was still one more very important number pattern to be realized. On the ***MATHEMATICAL FINGER PRINT OF GOD***

Notice how the 3, 9, and 6 is in red and does not connect at the base. That is because it is a vector. The 1,2,4,8,7,5 is the third dimension while the oscillation between the 3 and 6 demonstrates the fourth dimension, which is the higher dimensional magnetic field of an electrical coil. The 3, 9, and 6 always occur together with the 9 as the control. In fact, the Yin/Yang is not a duality but rather a trinity. This is because the 3 and 6 represent each side of the Yin/Yang and the 9 is the "S" curve between them. Everything is based on thirds. We think that the universe is based on dualities because we see the effects not the cause.

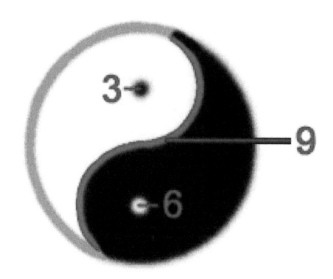

THE NUMBER 108 [9] - Moon

The 108 is another way of expressing the number 9 the number of enlightenment. See later Tesla and the 3, 6, 9.

Here are some spiritual and scientific meaning and facts attributed to the number 108:

The wholeness of existence – Renowned mathematicians of Vedic culture viewed 108 as the number of the wholeness of existence. Astronomically, there are 27 constellations in our galaxy and each has 4 directions. 27 x 4 = 108. In other words, the number 108 covers the whole galaxy.

Sun, Moon & Earth

The distance between the Earth and the Sun is 108 times the diameter of the Sun.

The distance between the Earth and Moon is 108 times the diameter of the Moon.

The diameter of the Sun is 108 times the diameter of the Earth. Silver is 108g / mole and associated with moon. One day is 86,400 seconds and the diameter of the sun is 864,000. Thus the second is related to the sun. The moon is 400 times smaller than the sun but 400 times closer to the earth. The earth moves 400 times faster than the moon.

Earth, Time and Body connection – Just like a circle, the Planet has 360° and each degree is divided into 60 minutes. One of these minutes' accounts for one nautical mile. That means the circumference of the Earth at the Equator is 21,600 nautical miles. On average, we take this many breaths a day. This connects our human body with the planet.

108

Mala Bead/Prayer Beads – In Hinduism and Buddhism, a mala comes as a string of 108 beads plus one guru or guiding bead. (A mala is like a Catholic rosary and is used for counting as you repeat a mantra.)

The Chakras are the intersections of energy lines, and there are said to be a total of 108 energy lines converging to form the heart chakra. One of them, sushumna leads to the crown chakra, and is said to be the path to Self-realization.

23

'Harshad' Number is an integer divisible by the sum of its digits. 108 is a 'Harshad' number. 'Harshad' in Sanskrit means 'joy-giver.'

Meditation – There are believed to be 108 different types of meditation.

Paths to God – Some people believe that there are 108 paths to God.

Dance Forms – There are 108 traditional Indian dance forms. (Traditional Indian dances are used to worship God or tell stories of God.)

In Buddhism, there are said to be 108 earthly desires in mortals, 108 lies humans tell and 108 human delusions.

108 feelings – Buddhist believe there are 108 feelings calculated as follows:

6 Senses (Smell, Touch, Taste, Sight, Hearing and Consciousness)

X 3 Pleasant, Painful or Neutral feelings

X 2 internally or externally generated feelings

X 3 Past, Present or Future feelings

Therefore, 36 past, 36 present and 36 future feelings = 108

In Yoga, 108 Sun Salutations are often practiced to honour change. Tibetans have 108 sacred holy books.

In Jainism, there are believed to be 108 virtues.

108 Steps – Many Hindu and Buddhist temples have 108 steps.

In Japan, at the end of a year, a bell is chimed 108 times in Buddhist temples to finish the old year and welcome the new one. Each ring represents one of the 108 earthly temptations a person must overcome to achieve nirvana.

Lord Buddha is believed to have given a teaching answering 108 questions which are contained within the Lankavatara Sutra (Buddhist scripture).

In Gnosticism, (an ancient Christian religion), it is believed that an individual has 108 chances, or lifetimes to eliminate ego and transcend the material world.

Atman/Soul – In Hinduism, it is believed that the soul or inner self (Atman), goes through 108 stages of spiritual development.

In Taoism, the Wu style of Tai Chi has 108 postures.

Lord Buddha's footprint is imprinted with 108 auspicious illustrations.

In Islam, the number 108 refers to God.

In the Bible, the word's 'first born' is used 108 times. The words 'in truth' and 'to forgive' are used 108 times in the New Revised Standard Version of the Bible.

Angel Numbers – the number 108 is a message of support and encouragement. A cycle in life might be coming to an end but new opportunities lay ahead.

1 = New beginnings, intuition, insight.

0 = Development of one's spiritual journey and listening to your intuition.

8 = Manifesting positive abundance, personal power, a desire for peace and a love of humanity.

The Sanskrit Alphabet has 54 letters and each has a masculine and feminine form (Shiva and Shakti) 54 x 2 = 108

Stonehenge, a prehistoric monument in England is 108 feet in diameter.

There is a lot of consider here and taking all of this into account, with a simplistic viewpoint, you could say that the auspicious number 108 connects science with human mind, body and spirit.

According to our Vedic cosmology, 108 is the basis of all creation.

It is the representation of our existence and our universe as a whole. This is properly exemplified when we try to understand the basis behind each number: the number 'one' signifies God's consciousness, the number 'zero' signifies null or void, while the number 'eight' is the embodiment of infinity. In short, the number 108 is everything that we are about.

The number's connection to astronomy.

In Vedic cosmology (and modern science), it is believed that the distance between the earth and the sun is 108 times the diameter of the sun, while the distance between the earth and the moon is 108 times the diameter of the moon. Furthermore, the diameter of the sun is 108 times that of the earth.

And the Sanskrit language has 54 alphabets. And when you multiply 54 and 2, you're left with the product 108.

The number 108 holds special importance in Hindu astrology, too.

According to the norms laid down by Hindu astrology, there are 12 rashis or zodiacs and 9 navagrahas or planets. So, if one multiplies the total number of zodiacs and the planets, the product is 108. Furthermore, there are 27 nakshatras or Lunar Mansions, which are further divided into 4 quarters or padas. Now, if you again multiply these two numbers, you get the auspicious number of 108 as the product.

One of the world's most famous prehistoric monuments, the Sarsen Circle Stonehenge, has a diameter of 108 feet.

Despite it being located in the UK, which is very, very far away from Asia, each column of the Stonehenge is surprisingly similar to PhNom Bakheng – an ancient Shiva temple in Cambodia and also a symbolic representation of Mount Meru. Surprisingly (or not, after reading this article), this temple has 108 adorning towers.

Jean Filliozat of the Ecole Francaise, French expert on Indian cosmology and astronomy, revealed a deep symbolical meaning hidden in PhNom Bakheng.

Concentrating on the portion that deals with the number 108, it has been found out that the temple is decorated with 108 surrounding towers with the central one representing the axis of the world and the 108 smaller ones represent the four lunar phases, each with 27 days. The seven levels of the monument represent the seven heavens and each terrace contains 12 towers which represent the 12-year cycle of Jupiter.

O.T.O (Ordo Templi Oreintis)

The numbers >> 111,222,333,444,555,666,777,888 and 999 all divide by 37. 3+7 =10. The 1 is the Holy Spirit and 0 is God. A circle 0 has 360 degrees 3+6+0 = 9; divide it 1+8+0 = 9. The 9 is both the source and also the vacuum thanks to duality. Keep dividing it will always add up to 9 22.5 = 2+2+5=9.

Any number multiplied by 9 and then add numbers you will get 9. Tesla shows how the 3, 6 and 9 created the quantum universe.

All secret societies know that numbers are encoded within language with patterns like Fibonacci sequence in nature which has a binary code hidden within the sequence.

The LOGOS for OTO is two triangles one going up and the other down like the Star of David. This represents the idea of "as above so below".

In centre of these triangles is a 5 leaf clover. As above so below is a Hermetic principle. See Kybalion for more understanding of Hermetic's.

Thus when you look at our galaxy you are seeing the universe and cells within oneself.

A bird's wings go up and down and the heart is in the centre of the bird. The wings are the triangles and the heart is our emotions.

The Bible tells us you have waters above and below the firmament. Firmament means fixed in place. The waters are like putting two mirrors facing each other. What results is a perception of infinity but it is not infinity. Ment means the mind from Latin. The firmament is also a vault. So perception of infinity is kept within the mind and consciousness of man.

Ordo means Order / Pattern / Structure /arrangement / Blueprint it hints at an intelligent source a Grand Architect of our universe.

Templi means Temple which is our human body which houses the Soul (Sol) the Sun.

Orient is the East where our sun rises. Orient also refers to how we orient ourselves when we prey. We normally face the Sun. The sun gives energy to plants which we eat and thus we get energy from the source of creation.

We are thus a fractal of god as man was created in his image. A hand has 14 sections. Add numbers 1 to 14 and you get 105.

The 5 leaf clover symbol in the centre of the OTO LOGOS is a way of showing the hand of God.

A	B	C	D	E	F	G	H	I	J
1	2	3	4	5	6	7	6	5	4
K	L	M							
3	2	1							
N	O	P	Q	R	S	T	U	V	W
1	2	3	4	5	6	7	6	5	4
X	Y	Z							
3	2	1							

Cipher of OTO above how numerals represent letters.

The Zodiac moves 1 degree every 72 years. 72 names are used in the Bible for God.

360 x 72 = God x 72 = 25,920

The equinox of the galaxy turning is every 26,000 years. The Mayans new this and knew that 21/12/2012 was a new age – the Age of Aquarius. [See my book age of Aquarius].

Orient also means superior grade / value. This shows that mans true divinity is from the Source – God – The Sun.

We are all fallen angels as made of light that came from the sun.

The numerology if you add up numbers in "Order of the Oriental Templar's adds up to 105.

God is both 0 and 360 he is nothing and everything at the same time. God does not have a name just the Source or the All and is beyond human comprehension. He is not an old man with a grey beard.

At the Quantum level the universe seems to be made of Tetrahedron building blocks.

The shape of the Universe is also Tetrahedron. I would argue it is infinite and all that we observe is the volume increasing within this, like new galaxies being formed. The universe is not cooling down so this is evidence that the big bang idea is flawed.

Cracking the Illuminati Cipher

1	2	3	4	5	6	7	8	9
A	B	C	D	E	F	G	H	I
J	K	K	M	N	O	P	Q	R
S	T	U	V	W	X	Y	Z	

NUMBER 1

10 reduces to 1 [1+0] = 1

1 means top dog / king

MICROSOFT = 493961662 = 46 = 10 = 1

IRS = 991 = 19 = 10 =1

NUMBER 2

2 means enlightened / awake

JESUS = 15131 = 11 = 2

11 =2, 20 = 2, 29 = 11 = 2

GOLD = 7634 = 20 = 2

NUMBER 3

3 means bottom / low quality

KIA = 291 = 12 = 3

NUMBER 4

Number 4 is secret society related.

Taylor Swift wears a 13 = 4

CNN = 355 = 13 = 4

NUMBER 22

Number 22 is a warrior for God a number not liked by secret societies thus JFK assassinated on $22^{nd} - 11 - 1963$.

NUMBER 5

Number 5 means unbalanced / war /deceit / asleep / dead / Masonic compass / lies.

Wizard of Oz a master Masonic film with controller controlling behind the curtain.

OZ = 68 = 14 = 5

NUMBER 6

Number 6 means illuminated / Secret Society member.

33 rites in Freemasonry

33 = 6

EBAY =6

DELL =6

E ON DELL IS AT ANGLE FOR E-COMMERCE

E = 5 = DECEIT

NUMBER 7

It is a neutral number so can be used for good or evil. It is the number of Isis.

Also represents the Masonic G

GOOGLE = 7

7 = Shiva

7 no of Chakras

NUMBER 8

8 represents the infinity of God.

8 represents balance / harmony.

NUMBER 9

9 is The End / Evil / Calculating

VW = 45 = 9

A phrase with 5 syllables like ABRACADABRA causes unbalance. It is used in Neuro linguistic programming along with colours / music and other techniques to affect your sub conscious mind. [The purpose to stop you becoming enlightened and remaining in the dark /dead]

911

This is the best message secret society members like to communicate with fellow members.

9 = TO END, 11 = THE AWAKENING

CONAN

CO = 36 =9

NAN = 515 =11

CONAN = 911

BRANDS

RAM = (9) 14 = 14 = 5

TO END - TO ATTACK

PEPSI = 75719 = 2 [9] = 11 [9] = 911

END THE AWAKENING

RED BULL

RED = 9

BULL = 2322 =11

END THE AWAKENING

KFC = 263 = 2 [9] = 119 = 911

5 SYLABLES IN MANY BRAND ADVERTS LIKE *VICTORIA SECRETS*

911 = destroy twin towers the eleven 11

STOP SOCIETY BEING ENLIGHTENED

6 =33 = MASONS

COCA-COLA = 3631-3631 = 13 – 13 = 4 - 4 = MASON – MASON

FACEBOOK =13 = 4 = MASON

MTV = MASON TV M =13 = 4 MADE AT MASONIC TEMPLE

8 IS THE INFINITY SIGN IT SHOWS GODS RELATIONSHIP TO MAN

	N1				N2	N1+N2
1X8	= 8	= Z		A	1	= 9
2X8	16[7]	= Y		B	2	= 9
3X8	24[6]	= X		C	3	= 9
4X8	32[5]	= W		D	4	= 9
5X8	40[4]	= V		E	5	= 9
6X8	48[12][3]	= U		F	6	= 9
7X8	56[11][2]	= T		G	7	= 9
8X8	64[10][1]	= S		H	8	= 9

The number zero is symbolic of God as God is everything and nothing /infinite and timeless.

The number 8 represents infinity but mans quickest route to God.

6 represent descending from heaven and 9 rising back to heaven after death or through meditation. [See my book Christ is within that covers the sacred oil – Christ means oil]

If we reverse the English language the original Hebrew language was read opposite to English from Right to left. If we then start off

With the letter Z and MULTIPLY BY 8 we get 8.

ADD THIS TO FIRST LETTER OF ALPHABET A =1 WE GET 9. TESLA KNEW THAT 9 WAS THE NUMBER OF ENLIGHTENMENT. NOT ONLY IS OUR DNA ENCODED BY GOD BUT ALSO OUR ENGLISH LANGUAGE AS EVERYTHING ADDS TO 9. The Akashic field contains recordings of all our thoughts in this lifetime. Zen Buddhists believe we are all Buddha's.

All is Tao thus the Godhead is everywhere but God is not within all. As only living things with DNA contain the Divinity of God hidden in this code. We are like a star our body can make internal light which we see in dreams etc. The Godhead sees the Universe though all its creations. We are just a fractal of the Godhead. There is no you or me just unity.

THE PLAN FOR 3 WORLD WARS

PIKE WAS BORN BEFORE WORLD WAR 1.

The following is a letter that speculation claimed that Albert Pike wrote to Giuseppe Mazzini in 1871 regarding a conspiracy involving three world wars that were planned in an attempt to take over the world.

The Pike letter to Giuseppe Mazzini was on display in the British Museum Library in London until 1977.

This letter has been claimed by many internet sites to reside in the British Library in London, which denies the letter exists.

Giuseppe Mazzini was an Italian revolutionary leader of the mid 1800s as well as the Director of the Illuminati

Albert Pike (historical Masonic figure) is a 33rd degree, Freemason Occultist Grand Master and creator of the Southern Jurisdiction of the Masonic Scottish Rite Order.

Following are apparently extracts from the letter, showing how Three World Wars have been planned for many generations.

"The First World War must be brought about in order to permit the Illuminati to overthrow the power of the Tsars in Russia and of making that country a fortress of atheistic Communism. The divergences caused by the "agentur" (agents) of the Illuminati between the British and Germanic Empires will be used to foment this war. At the end of the war, Communism will be built and used in order to destroy the other governments and in order to weaken the religions."

"The Second World War must be fomented by taking advantage of the differences between the Fascists and the political Zionists. This war must be brought about so that Nazism is destroyed and that the political Zionism be strong enough to institute a sovereign state of Israel in Palestine. During the Second World War, International Communism must become strong enough in order to balance Christendom, which would be then restrained and held in check until the time when we would need it for the final social cataclysm."

"The Third World War must be fomented by taking advantage of the differences caused by the "agentur" of the "Illuminati" between the political Zionists and the leaders of Islamic World. The war must be conducted in such a way that Islam (the Moslem Arabic World) and political Zionism (the State of Israel) mutually destroy each other.

Meanwhile the other nations, once more divided on this issue will be constrained to fight to the point of complete physical, moral, spiritual and economical exhaustion. We shall unleash the Nihilists and the atheists, and we shall provoke a formidable social cataclysm which in all its horror will show clearly to the nations the effect of absolute atheism, origin of savagery and of the bloodiest turmoil.

Then everywhere, the citizens, obliged to defend themselves against the world minority of revolutionaries, will exterminate those destroyers of civilization, and the multitude, disillusioned with Christianity, whose deistic spirits will from that moment be without compass or direction, anxious for an ideal, but without knowing where to render its adoration, will receive the true light through the universal manifestation of the pure doctrine of Lucifer, brought finally out in the public view.

This manifestation will result from the general reactionary movement which will follow the destruction of Christianity and atheism, both conquered and exterminated at the same time."

Pike was born in Boston, Massachusetts, son of Ben and Sarah (Andrews) Pike, and spent his childhood in Byfield and Newburyport, Massachusetts.

History of the Illuminati

The Illuminati trace their origins back thousands of years to their conception as a result of the genetic inbreeding between a reptilian extraterrestrial race and humanity. My research shows that the 3 Anunnaki Gods the Sumerians worshipped are just stars in the Triangulum Constellation [Enki, Enlil and Ea]. This constellation is found by following Pisces [fish] to Capricorn [ram]. This was the so called period Jesus lived in. It is all Astro-theology. [see my book when Saturn ruled the Sky]

Their modern origin, however, traces back to the 1760s and a man named Adam Weishaupt, who defected from the Catholic Church and organized the Illuminati, financed by the International Bankers mainly Zionists. Since then, according to the Illuminati, their top goal has been to achieve a "one world government" and to subjugate all religions and governments in the process. The Illuminati thus attribute all wars since the French Revolution as having been fomented by them in their pursuit of their goals.

Weishaupt wrote out a master plan in the 1770s outlining the Illuminati's goals, finishing on May 1, 1776. According to the Illuminati, this great day is still commemorated by Communist nations in the form of May Day. At the time Weishaupt's ideology was first introduced, Britain and France were the two greatest world powers, and so the Illuminati claimed credit for having kindled the Revolutionary War in order to weaken the British Empire and the French Revolution to destroy the French Empire. The French Revolution was a ruse to free the Maquis De Sade a perverted Illuminati member.

In the 1780s, the Bavarian Government found out about the Illuminati's subversive activities, forcing the Illuminati to disband and go underground. For the next few decades, the Illuminati operated under various names and guises, still in active pursuit of their ultimate goal. According to the Illuminati, the Napoleonic Wars were a direct result of Illuminati intervention, and were intended to weaken the governments of Europe. One of the results of these wars was the "Congress of Vienna", supposedly brought about by the Illuminati who then attempted to form a one world government in the form of a "League of Nations." However, Russia held out and the League of Nations was not formed, causing great animosity towards the Russian government on the part of the Illuminati.

The Illuminati contend that they have achieved control over the world's economy by controlling the International Bankers in their effort to create a one world government. It was the Rothschild's dynasty that instructed Weishaupt to set up the illuminati. All Vatican money is held in

41

Rothschild banks. Rothschild's used to set the Gold price. They control the Federal Reserve, City of London, Washington DC, are in union with the Jesuits and Black Pope and Black nobility.

Their short-term plan foiled, the Illuminati adopted a different strategy. The Illuminati say that they achieved control over the European economy through the International Bankers and directed the composition of Karl Marx's Communist Manifesto and its anti-thesis written by Karl Ritter in order to use the differences between the two ideologies to enable them to "divide larger and larger members of the human race into opposing camps so that they could be armed and then brainwashed into fighting and destroying each other."

Under new leadership by an American general named Albert Pike, the Illuminati worked out a blueprint for three world wars throughout the 20th century that would lead to a one world government by the end of the 20th century. According to the Illuminati, the First World War was fought to destroy Czarism in Russia (the Illuminati had held a grudge against the Czarist regime since Russia had thwarted its plans for a one world government after the Napoleonic Wars) and to establish Russia as a stronghold of Communism.

Likewise, the Illuminati claim that the Second World War pitted the Fascists against the "political Zionists" so as to build up International Communism until it equalled in strength that of the United Christendom. According to Illuminati plans, the Third World War, which is to be fought between the political Zionists and the leaders of the Moslem world, will drain the international community to the extent that they will have no choice but to form a one world government.

The Illuminati are an international group whose primary goal is the control of the entire world under a one world government. They believe that their "centre of power" is in the lower fourth dimension, the lower astral as many people call it, the traditional home for the 'demons' of folklore and myth.

Divide and Conquer

The Illuminati tactic is to divide and conquer by supplying arms and money to both sides and instigating people to fight and kill each other in order to be able to achieve their objectives. They foster the terrorism of atomic warfare [all those involved in the Manhattan Atomic bomb development were Jews] and deliberately cause world famine. In pursuit of their primary goal of a one world government, they plan to destroy all religions and governments in the process.

An Ex Freemason speaks as follows:-

I am a Past Master of a Freemason's Lodge which is affiliated with the Grand Lodge of New Zealand. Like all Masons, we are part of the Illuminati - but this is one of our secrets, which we've been keeping since 1599, when we were reincarnated out of the remnants of the Knights Templars.

Unfortunately, somehow, over the last 418 years, the profane - that is our term for those not in the know - have learned some of our secrets, and what we have been up to.

Why, some of them assert they are more in the know than even us senior members of The Craft. That is another term we try not to let out. Just how the profane know they know and we don't is a mystery, but we do have Brethren on the case. Woe to them if we find out.

So, for 418 years, we have been setting up the New World Order, and we're going to run it with our One World Government. And then it will be all up for you lot, forever and ever.

The Year 1785 - Germany

1785 – An Illuminati courier named Lanze is struck by lightning, and killed while travelling by horseback : Ratisbon. Bavarian officials examine the contents of his saddle bags, discovering the existence of the Order of the Illuminati, and find plans detailing the coming French Revolution. Bavarian officials arrest all members of the Illuminati they can find, but Weishaupt and others have gone underground, and cannot be found.

1796 – Freemasonry becomes a major issue in the presidential election in the United States.

1773 – Mayer Amschel Rothschild assembles twelve of his most influential friends, and convinces them that if they all pool their resources together, they can rule the world. This meeting takes place in Frankfurt, Germany.

Rothschild also informs his friends that he has found the perfect candidate, an individual of incredible intellect and ingenuity, to lead the organization he has planned – Adam Weishaupt. May 1, 1776 – Adam Weishaupt (code named Spartacus) establishes a secret society called the Order of the Illuminati. Weishaupt is the Professor of Canon Law at the University of Ingolstadt in Bavaria, part of Germany. The Illuminati seek to establish a New World Order. See my book The Puppet Master for more on Illuminati members.

Their objectives are as follows:

1) Abolition of all ordered governments
2) Abolition of private property
3) Abolition of inheritance
4) Abolition of patriotism
5) Abolition of the family
6) Abolition of religion
7) Creation of a world government

July, 1782 – The Order of the Illuminati joins forces with Freemasonry at the Congress of Wilhelmsbad. The Comte de Virieu, an attendee at the conference, comes away visibly shaken. When questioned about the "tragic secrets" he brought back with him, he replies:

From this time on, according to his biographer, "the Comte de Virieu could only speak of Freemasonry with horror."

The insignia of the Order of the Illuminati first appeared on the reverse side of U.S. one-dollar bills in 1933. One can read, at the base of the 13-story pyramid, the year 1776 (MDCCLXVI in Roman numerals). The eye radiating in all directions is the "all-spying eye" that symbolizes the terroristic, Gestapo-like, agency set up by Weishaupt.

The Latin words "ANNUIT COEPTIS" mean "our enterprise (conspiracy) has been crowned with success." Below, "NOVUS ORDO SECLORUM" explains the nature of the enterprise: a "New Social Order" or a "New World Order".

1797 – John Robison, Professor of Natural History at Edinburgh University in Scotland, publishes a book entitled "Proofs of a Conspiracy" in which he reveals that Adam Weishaupt had attempted to recruit him. He exposes the diabolical aims of the Illuminati to the world.

1821 – George W. F. Hegel formulates what is called the Hegelian dialectic – the process by which Illuminati objectives are achieved. According to the Hegelian dialectic, thesis plus antithesis equals synthesis. In other words, first you foment a crisis. Then there is an enormous public outcry that something must be done about the problem. So you offer a solution that brings about the changes you really wanted all along, but which people would have been unwilling to accept initially.

1828 – Mayer Amschel Rothschild, who finances the Illuminati, expresses his utter contempt for national governments which attempt to regulate International Bankers such as him:

"Allow me to issue and control the money of a nation, and I care not who writes the laws."

1848 — Moses Mordecai Marx Levy, alias Karl Marx, writes "The Communist Manifesto." Marx is a member of an Illuminati front organization called the League of the Just.

He not only advocates economic and political changes; he advocates moral and spiritual changes as well. He believes the family should be abolished, and that all children should be raised by a central authority. He expresses his attitude toward God by saying:

"We must war against all prevailing ideas of religion, of the state, of country, of patriotism. The idea of God is the keynote of a perverted civilization. It must be destroyed."

Jan. 22, 1870 – In a letter to Italian revolutionary leader Giuseppe Mazzini, Albert Pike – announces the establishment of a secret society within a secret society:

"We must create a super rite, which will remain unknown, to which we will call those Masons of high degree of whom we shall select. With regard to our brothers in Masonry, these men must be pledges to the strictest secrecy. Through this supreme rite, we will govern all Freemasonry which will become the one international centre, the more powerful because its direction will be unknown."

This ultra-secret organization is called The New and Reformed Palladian Rite. (This is why about 95% of the men involved in Masonry don't have a clue as to what the objectives of the organization actually are. They are under the delusion that it's just a fine community organization doing good works.)

1884 – The Fabian Society is founded in Great Britain to promote Socialism. The Fabian Society takes its name from the Roman General Fabius Maximus, who fought Hannibal's army in small debilitating skirmishes, rather than attempting one decisive battle.

July 14, 1889 – Albert Pike issues instructions to the 23

Supreme Councils of the world. He reveals who is the true object of Masonic worship:

"To you, Sovereign Grand Instructors General, we say this, that you may repeat it to the Brethren of the 32nd, 31st and 30th degrees: The Masonic religion should be, by all of us initiates of the high degrees, maintained in the purity of the Luciferian doctrine."

Lucifer was invented by Milton as a fallen Angel in the Epic "Paradise Lost". Milton got the idea for this epic by reading the book of Enoch and Sumerian legends. Lucifer also means light bearer. The illuminati mean the illumination within when they refer to Lucifer not the Devil. Satan has route from Sumerian myths. The Egyptians called the night Set. For Egyptians the underworld was just the Southern Hemisphere.

1890-1896 – Cecil Rhodes, an enthusiastic student of John Ruskin, is Prime Minister of South Africa, a British colony at the time. He is able to exploit and control the gold and diamond wealth of South Africa. He works to bring all the habitable portions of the world under the domination of ruling elite. To that end, he uses a portion of his vast wealth to establish the famous Rhodes Scholarships.

1911 – The Socialist Party of Great Britain publishes a pamphlet entitled "Socialism and Religion" in which they clearly state their position on Christianity:

"It is therefore a profound truth that Socialism is the natural enemy of religion. A Christian Socialist is in fact an anti-Socialist. Christianity is the antithesis of Socialism."

Feb. 3, 1913 – The 16th Amendment to the U.S. Constitution, making it possible for the Federal Government to impose a progressive income tax, is ratified. Plank #2 of "The Communist Manifesto" had called for a progressive income tax.

Dec. 23, 1913 – The Federal Reserve (neither federal nor a reserve – it's a privately owned institution) is created. It was planned at a secret meeting in 1910 on Jekyl Island, Georgia, by a group of bankers and politicians, including Col. House.

This transfers the power to create money from the American Government to a private group of bankers. The Federal Reserve Act is hastily passed just before the Christmas break. Congressman Charles A. Lindbergh Sr. (father of the famed aviator) warns:

"This act establishes the most gigantic trust on earth. When the President signs this act the invisible government by the money power, proven to exist by the Money Trust Investigation, will be legalized."

1916 – Three years after signing the Federal Reserve Act into law, President Woodrow Wilson observes:

"I am a most unhappy man. I have unwittingly ruined my country. A great industrial nation is controlled by its system of credit. Our system of credit is concentrated. The growth of the nation, therefore, and all our activities are in the hands of a few men. We have come to be one of the worst ruled, one of the most completely controlled and dominated governments in the civilized world. No longer a government by free opinion, no longer a government by conviction and the vote of the majority, but a government by the opinion and duress of a small group of dominant men."

1917 – With aid from Financiers in New York City and London, V. I. Lenin is able to overthrow the government of Russia. Lenin later comments on the apparent contradiction of the links between prominent capitalists and Communism:

"There also exists another alliance – at first glance a strange one, a surprising one – but if you think about it, in fact, one which is well grounded and easy to understand. This is the alliance between our Communist leaders and your capitalists."

(Remember the Hegelian dialectic?)

1920 – Britain's Winston Churchill recognizes the connection between the Illuminati and the Bolshevik Revolution in Russia.

51

Winston Churchill says:

"From the days of Spartacus-Weishaupt to those of Karl Marx, to those of Trotsky, Bela Kun, Rosa Luxembourg, and Emma Goldman, this world-wide conspiracy for the overthrow of civilization and for the reconstitution of society on the basis of arrested development, of envious malevolence and impossible equality, has been steadily growing.

It played a definitely recognizable role in the tragedy of the French Revolution. It has been the mainspring of every subversive movement during the nineteenth century, and now at last these bands of extra- ordinary personalities from the underworld of the great cities of Europe and America have gripped the Russian people by the hair of their heads, and have become practically the undisputed masters of that enormous empire."

1920-1931 – Louis T. McFadden is Chairman of the House Committee on Banking and Currency. Concerning the Federal Reserve, Congressman McFadden notes:

"When the Federal Reserve Act was passed, the people of these United States did not perceive that a world banking system was being set up here. A super-state controlled by International Bankers and international industrialists acting together to enslave the world for their own pleasure.

Every effort has been made by the Fed to conceal its powers, but the truth is – the Fed has usurped the

Government. It controls everything here, and it controls all our foreign relations. It makes and breaks governments at will." Concerning the Great Depression and the country's acceptance of FDR's New Deal, he asserts: "It was no accident. It was a carefully contrived occurrence. The International Bankers sought to bring about a condition of despair here so they might emerge as the rulers of us all."

1921 – Col. House reorganizes the American branch of the Institute of International Affairs into the Council on Foreign Relations (CFR). (For the past 60 years, 80% of the top positions in every administration – whether Democrat or Republican – have been occupied by members of this organization.)

December 15, 1922 – The CFR endorses World Government in its magazine "Foreign Affairs." Author Philip Kerr states:

"Obviously there is going to be no peace nor prosperity for mankind as long as the earth remains divided into 50 or 60 independent states, until some kind of international system is created. The real problem today is that of world government."

1928 – "The Open Conspiracy: Blue Prints for a World Revolution" by H. G. Wells is published. A former Fabian socialist, Wells writes:

"The political world of the Open Conspiracy must weaken, efface, incorporate, and supersede existing governments. The character of the Open Conspiracy will now be plainly displayed. It will be a world religion."

1933 – "The Shape of Things to Come" by H. G. Wells is published. Wells predicts a second world war around 1940, originating from a German-Polish dispute. After 1945, there would be an increasing lack of public safety in "criminally infected" areas.

The plan for the "Modern World State" would succeed on its third attempt, and come out of something that occurred in Basra, Iraq. The book also states:

"Although world government had been plainly coming for some years, although it had been endlessly feared and murmured against, it found no opposition anywhere."

Nov. 21, 1933 – In a letter to Col. Edward M. House, President Franklin Roosevelt writes:

"The real truth of the matter is, as you and I know that a financial element in the larger centres has owned the Government since the days of Andrew Jackson."

A meeting of the top officials of the council comes out in favour of:

1) a world government of delegated powers;
2) strong immediate limitations on national sovereignty;
3) international control of all armies and navies.
Representatives (375 of them) of 30-some denominations assert that "a new order of economic life is both imminent and imperative" – a new order that is sure to come either "through voluntary cooperation within the framework of democracy or through explosive revolution."

June 28, 1945 – U.S. President Harry Truman endorses world government in a speech:

"It will be just as easy for nations to get along in a republic of the world as it is for us to get along in a republic of the United States."

October 24, 1945 – The United Nations Charter becomes effective. Also on October 24, Senator Glen Taylor (D-Idaho) introduces Senate Resolution 183, calling upon the U.S. Senate to go on record as favouring creation of a world republic, including an international police force.

Feb. 7, 1950 – International financier and CFR member James Warburg tells a Senate Foreign Relations Subcommittee:

"We shall have world government whether or not you like it – by conquest or consent."

Feb. 9, 1950 – The Senate Foreign Relations Subcommittee introduces Senate Concurrent Resolution #66 which begins:

"Whereas, in order to achieve universal peace and justice, the present Charter of the United Nations should be changed to provide a true world government constitution."

1952 – The World Association of Parliamentarians for World Government draws up a map designed to illustrate how foreign troops would occupy and police the six regions into which the United States and Canada will be divided as part of their world-government plan.

1954 – Prince Bernhard of the Netherlands establishes the Bilderburgers: international politicians and bankers who meet secretly on an annual basis.

The United Nations detail a three-stage plan to disarm all nations and arm the U.N. with the final stage in which "no state would have the military power to challenge the progressively strengthened U.N. Peace Force."

1966 – Professor Carroll Quigley, Bill Clinton's mentor at Georgetown University, authors a massive volume entitled "Tragedy and Hope" in which he states:

"There does exist and has existed for a generation, an international network which operates, to some extent, in the

56

way the radical right believes the Communists act. In fact, this network, which we may identify as the Round Table Groups, has no aversion to cooperating with the Communists, or any other groups, and frequently does so.

I know of the operations of this network because I have studied it for twenty years and was permitted for two years, in the early 1960s, to examine its papers and secret records. I have no aversion to it or to most of its aims, and have, for much of my life, been close to it and too many of its instruments. I have objected, both in the past and recently, to a few of its policies, but in general my chief difference of opinion is that it wishes to remain unknown, and I believe its role in history is significant enough to be known."

April 1972 – In his keynote address to the Association for Childhood Education International, Chester M. Pierce, Professor of Education and Psychiatry in the Faculty of Medicine at Harvard University, proclaims:

"Every child in America entering school at the age of five is insane because he comes to school with certain allegiances toward our founding fathers, toward his parents, toward a belief in a supernatural being. It's up to you, teachers, to make all of these sick children well by creating the international child of the future."

July 1973 – International banker and staunch member of the subversive Council on Foreign Relations, David Rockefeller, founds a new organization called the Trilateral

Commission, of which the official aim is "to harmonize the political, economic, social, and cultural relations between the three major economic regions in the world" (hence the name "Trilateral").

There are three major economic areas in the world: Europe, North America, and the Far East (Japan, South Korea, Taiwan, etc.).
If, under the pretext of having to join forces to be able to face economic competition with the two other economic regions, the member countries of each of these three regions decide to merge into one single country, forming three super-States, then the one-world government will be almost achieved.

Like Fabian socialists, they achieve their ultimate goal (a world government) step by step. The Fabian society was a group of intellectuals studying the future of society. They included writers like George Orwell who wrote "1984" about Big Brother. Another Fabian member Aldous Huxley wrote "Brave New World".
This aim is almost achieved in Europe with the Single European Act (Maastricht Treaty) that was implemented in 1993, requiring all the member countries of the European Community to abolish their trade barriers, and to hand over their monetary and fiscal policies to the technocrats of the European Commission in Brussels, Belgium.

In January, 2002, all these European countries abandoned

their national currencies to share only one common currency, the "Euro". Moreover, the Nice Treaty removed more powers from countries to give them over to the European Commission.

What begun innocently in 1952 as the EEC (European Economic Community, a common authority to regulate the coal and steel industry among European nations), finally turned into a European super-state.

Jean Monnet, a French socialist economist and founder of the EEC, said: "Political union inevitably follows economic union." He also said in 1948:

"The creation of a United Europe must be regarded as an essential step towards the creation of a United World."

As regards the North American area, the merger of its member countries is well under way with the passage of free trade between Canada and the U.S.A., and then Mexico.

In the next few years, this free-trade agreement is supposed to include also all of South and Central America, with a single currency for them all.

Mexico's President Vucente Fox said on May 6, 2002, in Madrid:

"Eventually, our long-range objective is to establish with the United States, but also with Canada, our other regional partner, an ensemble of connections and institutions similar to those created by the European Union."

1973 – The Club of Rome, a U.N. operative, issues a report entitled "Regionalized and Adaptive Model of the Global World System." This report divides the entire world into ten kingdoms.

1979 – FEMA, which stands for the Federal Emergency Management Agency, is given huge powers. It has the power, in case of "national emergency", to suspend laws, move entire populations, arrest and detain citizens without a warrant, and hold them without trial.

It can seize property, food supplies, transportation systems, and can suspend the Constitution. Not only is it the most powerful entity in the United States, but it was not even created under Constitutional law by the Congress.

1991 – President George Bush Sr. praises the New World Order in a State of the Union Message:

"What is at stake is more than one small country; it is a big idea –"a new world order" to achieve the universal aspirations of mankind, based on shared principles and the rule of law. The illumination of a thousand points of light. The winds of change are with us now." (Theosophist Alice Bailey used that very same expression – "points of light" – in describing the process of occult enlightenment.)

60

June, 1991 – World leaders are gathered for another closed door meeting of the Bilderberg Society in Baden Baden, Germany. While at that meeting, David Rockefeller said in a speech:

"We are grateful to the Washington Post, The New York Times, Time Magazine and other great publications whose directors have attended our meetings and respected their promises of discretion for almost forty years. It would have been impossible for us to develop our plan for the world if we had been subjected to the lights of publicity during those years. But, the world is now more sophisticated and prepared to march towards a world government. The supranational sovereignty of an intellectual elite and world bankers is surely preferable to the national auto-determination practiced in past centuries."

Oct. 29, 1991 – David Funderburk, former U.S. Ambassador to Romania, tells a North Carolina audience:

"George Bush has been surrounding himself with people who believe in one-world government. They believe that the Soviet system and the American system are converging."

May 21, 1992 – In an address to the Bilderberg organization meeting in Evian, France, former Secretary of State Henry Kissinger declares:

"Today Americans would be outraged if U.N. troops entered Los Angeles to restore order; tomorrow they will be grateful! This is especially true if they were told there was an outside threat from beyond, whether real or promulgated, that threatened our very existence.

The Numbers 432 and 108

All music instruments used to be tuned to 432 Hertz but this was changed by the Rockefeller family to the value to 440 Hertz. 432 Hertz is good for mind, body and consciousness – see my book on using sound to heal. 440Hertz is bad for our health.

Number 432

TIME MEASURE	
⊙NE SOLAR DAY	= 24 HOURS
24 HRS X 60 MIN	= 1,440 MINUTES
1,440 MIN X 60 SEC	= 86,400 SECONDS
720 A HALF DAY MIN X 60 SEC	= 43,200 SECONDS

The Pyramid and Earth Radius

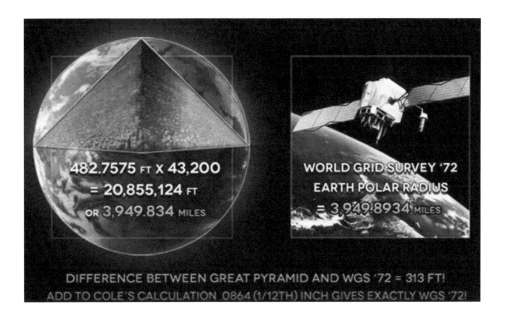

482.7575 FT X 43,200
= 20,855,124 FT
OR 3,949.834 MILES

WORLD GRID SURVEY '72
EARTH POLAR RADIUS
= 3,949.8934 MILES

DIFFERENCE BETWEEN GREAT PYRAMID AND WGS '72 = 313 FT!
ADD TO COLE'S CALCULATION .0864 (1/12TH) INCH GIVES EXACTLY WGS '72!

We can see from above that the Egyptians must have been able to work out what the Earths radius was. If you multiply the dimensions of the Pyramid by the number of seconds in half a day [43,200] then you get the polar Radius in miles.

THE PRE-DELUVIAN GOD KINGS OF SUMERIA

Name of King	Years of Reign
Aloros	36,000
Alaporos	10,800
Amelon	46,800
Ammenon	43,200
Megalaros	64,800
Daonos	36,000
Euedoroches	64,800
Amempsinos	36,000
Opartes	28,800
Xisuhtros	64,800
Total Years ➡	432,000

We can see from the above that the Total Years that Sumerian Gods ruled for is based on the number 432.

The Kali Yoga cycle began approximately 5,000 years ago and it has duration of 432,000 years. This gives us 427,000 years to the end of the present age. [See my book the Age of Aquarius This book covers great cycles known to ancient people on Earth.

The radius of the moon is 1,080 miles.

The radius of the Sun is 432,000 miles.

Did all this happen by chance so we see a perfect lunar eclipse?

Both numbers 1,080 and 432,000 add up to the 9.

A temple in Cambodia has 108 towers on it that look like pinecones.

May 1st

May 1st marks the beginning of spring the spring equinox. This day was also associated with Beltane (/ˈbɛl.teɪn/) is the anglicised name for the Gaelic May Day festival. Most commonly it is held on 1 May, or about halfway between the spring equinox and the summer solstice. Historically, it was widely observed throughout Ireland, Scotland and the Isle of Man. It marked the beginning of summer and was when cattle were driven out to the summer pastures. Rituals were performed to protect the cattle, crops and people, and to encourage growth. Special bonfires were kindled, and their flames, smoke and ashes were deemed to have protective powers. The people and their cattle would walk around the bonfire or between two bonfires, and sometimes leap over the flames or embers. All household fires would be doused and then re-lit from the Beltane bonfire. The word bonfire comes from bone fire where animal or human sacrifice was done and then victim burnt and bones read by the witch doctor. May 1st also linked with the worship of Ba'al and was the day in history when the illuminati founded and day communists celebrate the world over.

Arkana – Lesser

Minor
Consciousness
Small things
Microcosm
Monad

Arkana – Major

Macrocosm
Large
Laws of Nature
Universal Laws

Natural comes from Natur = Nectar = Spirits
And 'al' means 'of'
Occult means hidden or esoteric
Hidden because this knowledge is the power of how humans can be controlled and manipulated.
Nescience means not to know because information is absent.
Ignore – 'ance' means data and information is available and in front of you but you choose to IGNORE information as it does not agree with your view point. There is no excuse for IGNORANCE.

Dia-gnosis means the method to knowledge. Without knowledge you can't rectify the problem.

Perception is a filter yet truth not based on perception. You can't change the past. Truth only exists in the past or present moment not in the future.

10/3[trinity] = 3.333 to infinity.
7 = ethereal form
Zeus = Orion = God Consciousness

Tarot Cards

The Freemasons were entrusted in preserving the knowledge of the ancient mystery schools. They have failed in this task but the Gypsies preserved the secrets within symbolism – contained in their Tarot cards. See Papus – The Tarot of the Bohemians.

The Fool is Card 0 or 22.

Notice the feather in his hat this is symbolic of Orion the Sun that gives energy to our Spirit as shown top right. The fool is on a cliff which represents falling from heaven and away from divinity to our earthly realm. We can see the elements in the image and the dog is probably symbolic of the dog star.

The Magician is card number 1 – we can see the infinity symbol above his head showing that time is eternal. The scroll is unopened showing the Magician is not close to divinity.

The Empress is card number 2. We can see she is closer to divinity than the Magician as she holds the opened scroll. Picture above shows an orb in this case. She also has the crown on her head which is symbolic of being closer to God as it represents Kether on the Kabbalah Tree of Life. The Magician and Empress represent the Dualistic Nature of Creation – Man / Women.

The Legend of Osiris

Osiris the great-grandson of Ra sat upon the throne of the gods, ruling over the living world as Ra did over the gods. He was the first Pharaoh, and his Queen, Isis, was the first Queen. They ruled for many ages together, for the world was still young and Grandmother Death was not as harsh as she is now.

His ways were just and upright, he made sure that Maat remained in balance, that the law was kept. And so Maat smiled upon the world. All peoples praised Osiris and Isis, and peace reigned over all, for this was the Golden Age.

Yet there was trouble. Proud Set, noble Set, the brother of Osiris, he who defended the Sun Boat from Apep the Destroyer, was unsettled in his heart. He coveted the throne of Osiris. He coveted Isis. He coveted the power over the living world and he desired to take it from his brother. In his dark mind he conceived of a plot to kill Osiris and take all from him. He built a box and inscribed it with wicked magic that would chain anyone who entered it from escaping.

Set took the box to the great feast of the gods. He waited until Osiris had made himself drunk on beer, he then challenged Osiris to a contest of strength. Each one in turn would enter the box, and attempt, through sheer strength, to break it open. Osiris, sure in his power yet feeble in mind because of his drink, entered the box. Set quickly poured molten lead into the box. Osiris tried to escape, but the wicked magic held him bound and he died. Set then picked up the box and hurled it into the Nile where it floated away.

Set claimed the throne of Osiris for himself and demanded that Isis be his Queen. None of the other gods dared to stand against him, for he had killed Osiris and could easily do the same to them. Great Ra turned his head aside and mourned, he did not stand against Set.

This was the dark time. Set was everything his brother was not. He was cruel and unkind, caring not for the balance of Maat, or for us, the children of the gods. War divided Egypt, and all was lawless while Set ruled. In vain our people cried to Ra, but his heart was hardened by grief, and he would not listen.

Only Isis, blessed Isis, remembered us. Only she was unafraid of Set. She searched all of the Nile for the box containing her beloved husband. Finally she found it, lodged in a tamarisk bush that had turned into a mighty tree, for the power of Osiris still was in him, though he lay dead. She tore open the box and wept over the lifeless body of Osiris. She carried the box back to Egypt and placed it in the house of the gods. She changed herself into a bird and flew about his body, singing a song of mourning. Then she perched upon him and cast a spell. The spirit of dead Osiris entered her and she did conceive and bear a son whose destiny it would be to avenge his father. She called the child Horus, and hid him on an island far away from the gaze of his uncle Set.

She then went to Thoth, wise Thoth, who knows all secrets, and implored his help. She asked him for magic that could bring Osiris back to life. Thoth, lord of knowledge, who brought himself into being by speaking his name, searched through his magic. He knew that Osiris' spirit had departed his body and was lost. To restore Osiris, Thoth had to remake him so that his spirit would recognize him and rejoin. Thoth and Isis together created the Ritual of Life, that which allows us to live forever when we die. But before Thoth could work the magic, cruel Set discovered them. He stole the body of Osiris and tore it into many pieces, scattering them throughout Egypt. He was sure that Osiris would never be reborn.

Yet Isis would not despair. She implored the help of her sister Nephthys, kind Nephthys, to guide her and help her find the pieces of Osiris. Long did they search, bringing each piece to Thoth that he might work magic upon it. When all the pieces were together, Thoth went to Anubis, lord of the dead. Anubis sewed the pieces back together, washed the entrails of Osiris, embalmed him wrapped him in linen, and cast the Ritual of Life. When Osiris' mouth was opened, his spirit re-entered him and he lived again.

Yet nothing that has died, not even a god, may dwell in the land of the living. Osiris went to Duat, the abode of the dead. Anubis yielded the throne to him and he became the lord of the dead. There he stands in judgment over the souls of the dead. He commends the just to the Blessed Land, but the wicked he condemns to be devoured by Ammit.

When Set heard that Osiris lived again he was annoyed, but his anger waned, for he knew that Osiris could never return to the land of the living. Without Osiris, Set believed he would sit on the throne of the gods for all time. Yet on his island, Horus, the son of Osiris and Isis, grew to manhood and strength. Set sent many serpents and demons to kill Horus, but he defeated them. When he was ready, his mother Isis gave him great magic to use against Set, and Thoth gave him a magic knife.

Horus sought out Set and challenged him for the throne. Set and Horus fought for many days, but in the end Horus defeated Set and castrated him. But Horus, merciful Horus, would not kill Set, for to spill the blood of his uncle would make him no better than he. Set maintained his claim to the throne, and Horus lay claim himself as the son of Osiris. The gods began to fight amongst another, those who supported Horus and those who supported Set. Banebdjetet leaped into the middle and demanded that the gods end this struggle peacefully or Maat would be imbalanced further. He told the gods to seek the council of Neith. Neith, warlike though wise in council, told them that Horus was the rightful heir to the throne. Horus cast Set into the darkness where he lives to this day.

And so it is that Horus watches over us while we live, and gives guidance to the Pharaoh while he lives, and his father Osiris watches over us in the next life. So it is that the gods are at peace. So it is that Set, wicked Set, eternally strives for revenge, battling Horus at every turn. When Horus wins, Maat is upheld and the world is at peace. When Set wins, the world is in turmoil. But we know that dark times do not last forever, and the bright rays of Horus will shine over us again. In the last days, Horus and Set will fight one last time for the world. Horus will defeat Set forever, and Osiris will be able to return to this world. On that day, the Day of Awakening, all the tombs shall open and the just dead shall live again as we do, and all sorrow shall pass away forever.

Lo, this is my tale. Keep it in your hearts and give it to others, as I gave it to you.

Osiris / Apollo / Nimrod [He who rebelled], Gilgamesh, Chronus, Saturn, Molak are all the same names under different cultures and times.

Ra / Ba'al = Sun God

Set fooled Osiris into getting into a box, which Set then shut, sealed with lead, and threw into the Nile. Osiris' wife, Isis, searched for his remains until she finally found him embedded in a tamarisk tree trunk, which was holding up the roof of a palace in Byblos on the Phoenician coast. She managed to remove the coffin and open it, but Osiris was already dead.

In one version of the myth, she used a spell learned from her father and brought him back to life so he could impregnate her. Afterwards he died again and she hid his body in the desert. Months later, she gave birth to Horus. While she raised Horus, Set was hunting one night and came across the body of Osiris.

Enraged, he tore the body into fourteen pieces and scattered them throughout the land. Isis gathered up all the parts of the body, except the penis (which had been eaten by a fish, the medjed) and bandaged them together for a proper burial. The gods were impressed by the devotion of Isis and resurrected Osiris as the god of the underworld. Because of his death and resurrection, Osiris was associated with the flooding and retreating of the Nile and thus with the crops along the Nile valley.

Diodorus Siculus gives another version of the myth in which Osiris was described as an ancient king who taught the Egyptians the arts of civilization, including agriculture, then travelled the world with his sister Isis, the satyrs, and the nine muses, before finally returning to Egypt. Osiris was then murdered by his evil brother Typhon, who was identified with Set. Typhon divided the body into twenty-six pieces, which he distributed amongst his fellow conspirators in order to implicate them in the murder. Isis and Hercules (Horus) avenged the death of Osiris and slew Typhon. Isis recovered all the parts of Osiris' body, except the phallus, and secretly buried them. She made replicas of them and distributed them to several locations, which then became centres of Osiris worship.

Djed symbol holds up heavens in Egyptian mythology. Osiris is symbolic of Orisons belt. It is a piece of his spine. As Nimrod / Osiris has lost his penis thus phallic obelisks put on earth to worship Osiris / Nimrod cult.

The Djed pillar, an ancient Egyptian symbol meaning 'stability', is the symbolic backbone of the god Osiris.

The Djed may originally have been a fertility cult related pillar made from reeds or sheaves or a totem from which sheaves of grain were suspended or grain was piled around. Erich Neumann remarks that the Djed pillar is a tree fetish, which is significant considering that Egypt was primarily treeless. He indicates that the myth may represent the importance of the importation of trees by Egypt from Syria. The Djed came to be associated with Seker, the falcon god of the Memphite necropolis, then with Ptah, the Memphite patron god of craftsmen. Ptah was often referred to as "the noble Djed", and carried a sceptre that was a combination of the Djed symbol and the ankh, the symbol of life. Ptah gradually came to be assimilated into Osiris. By the time of the New Kingdom, the Djed was firmly associated with Osiris.

In their 2004 book The Quick and the Dead, Andrew Hunt Gordon and Calvin W. Schwabe speculated that the ankh, Djed, and was symbols have a biological basis derived from ancient cattle culture (linked to the Egyptian belief that semen was created in the spine), thus:

The Ankh, symbol of life, thoracic vertebra of a bull (seen in cross section).

The Djed, symbol of stability, base on sacrum of a bull's spine.

The Was, symbol of power and dominion, a staff featuring the head and tail of the god Set, "great of strength".

Babylonian Myths

Hammurabi (c. 1810 BC – c. 1750 BC) was the sixth king of the First Babylonian Dynasty, reigning from 1792 BC to 1750 BC (according to the Middle Chronology). He was preceded by his father, Sin-Muballit, who abdicated due to failing health.

Hammurabi was seen by many as a god within his own lifetime. After his death, Hammurabi was revered as a great conqueror that spread civilization and forced all peoples to pay obeisance to Marduk, the national god of the Babylonians. Later, his military accomplishments became de-emphasized and his role as the ideal lawgiver became the primary aspect of his legacy. For later Mesopotamians, Hammurabi's reign became the frame of reference for all events occurring in the distant past. Even after the empire he built collapsed, he was still revered as a model ruler, and many kings across the Near East claimed him as an ancestor. Hammurabi was rediscovered by archaeologists in the late nineteenth century and has since become seen as an important figure in the history of law.

In Mesopotamian mythology, Marduk was a Babylonian sky god who created the earth and sky from the body of the great dragon Tiamat, the mother of all beings.

Enlil, later known as Elil, was the ancient Mesopotamian god of wind, air, earth, and storms. He is first attested as the chief deity of the Sumerian pantheon,[but he was later worshipped by the Akkadians, Babylonians, Assyrians, and Hurrians. Enlil's primary centre of worship was the Ekur temple in the city of Nippur, which was believed to have been built by Enlil himself and was regarded as the "mooring-rope" of heaven and earth.

He is also sometimes referred to in Sumerian texts as Nunamnir.

Enlil rose to prominence during the twenty-fourth century BC with the rise of Nippur. His cult fell into decline after Nippur was sacked by the Elamites in 1230 BC and he was eventually supplanted as the chief god of the Mesopotamian pantheon by the Babylonian national god Marduk. The Babylonian god Bel was a syncretic deity of Enlil, Marduk, and the dying god Dumuzid.

79

Enlil plays a vital role in the Sumerian creation myth; he separates An (heaven) from Ki (earth), thus making the world habitable for humans. In the Sumerian Flood myth, Enlil rewards Ziusudra with immortality for having survived the flood and, in the Babylonian flood myth, Enlil is the cause of the flood himself, having sent the flood to exterminate the human race, which made too much noise and prevented him from sleeping.

Canaanite's

Moloch is the biblical name of a Canaanite god associated with child sacrifice. The name of this deity is also sometimes spelled Molech, Milcom, or Malcam.

John Dee

John Dee (13 July 1527 – 1608 or 1609) was an English mathematician, astronomer, astrologer, occult philosopher, and advisor to Queen Elizabeth I. He devoted much of his life to the study of alchemy, divination, and Hermetic philosophy. He was also an advocate of England's imperial expansion into a "British Empire", a term he is generally credited with coining.

Dee straddled the worlds of modern science and magic just as the former was emerging. One of the most learned men of his time; he had been invited to lecture on the geometry of Euclid at the University of Paris while still in his early twenties. Dee was an ardent promoter of mathematics and a respected astronomer, as well as a leading expert in navigation, having trained many of those who would conduct England's voyages of discovery.

Simultaneously with these efforts, Dee immersed himself in the worlds of magic, astrology and Hermetic philosophy. He devoted much time and effort in the last thirty years or so of his life to attempting to commune with angels in order to learn the universal language of creation and bring about the pre-apocalyptic unity of mankind. However, Robert Hooke suggested in the chapter Of Dr. Dee's Book of Spirits, that John Dee made use of Trithemian steganography, to conceal his communication with Elizabeth I. A student of the Renaissance Neo-Platonism of Marsilio Ficino, Dee did not draw distinctions between his mathematical research and his investigations into Hermetic magic, angel summoning and divination. Instead he considered all of his activities to constitute different facets of the same quest: the search for a transcendent understanding of the divine forms which underlie the visible world, which Dee called "pure verities".

In his lifetime, Dee amassed one of the largest libraries in England. His high status as a scholar also allowed him to play a role in Elizabethan politics. Many don't believe John Dee spoke to Angels but just invented a book of code to speak to the Queen with.

Jeremy Cross' "The Broken Column"

The broken column carefully laid on the third step of the base completes the symbolic legend of the Third Degree in Freemasonry.

The image consists of a weeping virgin, holding in one hand a sprig of acacia [acacia contains DMT] and in the other an urn; before her is a broken column, on which rests a copy of the Book of Constitutions, while Father Time behind her is attempting to disentangle the ringlets of her hair.

The broken column denotes the untimely death of our Grand Master Hiram Abiff also symbolic of the story of Osiris losing his penis; the beautiful virgin weeping, the temple unfinished; the book open before her, that his virtues lie on perpetual record; the sprig of acacia in her right hand, the timely discovery of his body; the urn in her left, that his ashes were then safely deposited to perpetuate the remembrance of so distinguished a character; Time unfolding the ringlets of her hair, that time, patience, and perseverance accomplish all things.

King Solomon used a secret word with a ritualistic grip to raise Hiram Abiff from the dead. Hiram Abiff the Master Mason was captured by the Jews to try and get him to give the secret code word that is built into the temple.

Ritual code to 923

1000 years before Christ.

M A	H A	BONE
13 1 8 1	2 15	14 5
14	8	10 [8+10 =18 =9]
23	- 9	

GIVES 9 -23 THE MASONIC HANDSHAKE OR THE LIONS GRIP

LIONS GRIP

The MA-HA-Bone is the real grip of the Master Mason. Mason grips the right hand of a fellow Mason. Thumbs on both hands interlaced [This is the 2]. The first Mason presses 3 of his fingers – 2 nearest thumb and then third finger has a gap between 2nd. He presses these fingers on wrist of fellow Mason where it unites with the hand. The second Mason then does the same.

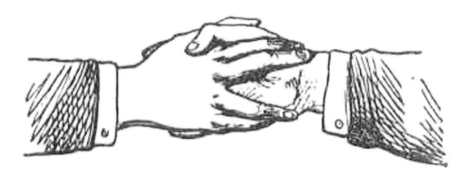

The Mason firmly grasps the right hand of a fellow Mason. The thumbs of both hands are interlaced. The first Mason presses the tops of his fingers against the wrist of the fellow Mason where it unites with the hand. The fellow Mason at the same time presses his fingers against the corresponding part of the first Mason's hand and the fingers of each are somewhat apart. This grip is also called the Strong Grip of the Master Mason or the Lion's Paw. Instruction for this grip is given at the "graveside", after the candidate has been "raised".

If you see the 5 each 6's in the fingers note this is 5 x 6 = 30. Thus number 30 in play. 30 was a measurement used in Solomon's temple.

84

What the 923 means?

9+2+3 = 14 these are the 14 pieces that Osiris was broken into. ISIS is the virgin is Virgo / Rhea / Mary.

Rhea is a character in Greek mythology, the Titaness daughter of the earth goddess Gaia and the sky god Uranus as well as sister and wife to Cronus.

Rhea presenting Cronus the stone wrapped in cloth. Thus we see a gift from the Virgin to father time. Have freemasons being manipulating time and is the Great Deception being going on since more than 1000 years before Christ? Were the Jews who wrote the Bible really working for the Masons?

Osiris / Nimrod rules the underworld is this why the Masons keep putting up Obelisks to Worship the Phallus that Osiris lost?

The King James Version (KJV) has been considered to be authoritative by many, but some modern translations are simpler. The New International Version (NIV) reads, "*He made the Sea of cast metal, circular in shape, measuring ten cubits from rim to rim and five cubits high. It took a line of thirty cubits to measure around it*". Footnotes for this verse indicate the length of a "*cubit*" to be about 1.5 feet.

A *cubit* is the distance from the elbow to the tip of the middle finger, although that definition begs the question of "whose forearm will we use?"

So the Bible states that this circular cast-metal (or "molten") basin (or "sea") had a diameter of 10 *cubits* and circumference of 30 *cubits*.

Solutions

Here are two solutions for the Temple of Solomon. The numbers in the Sower's parables in the Gospel, 30-60-100 or 100-60-30 unlock the Sower's Sevens.

Solution 1 in 1Kings chapters 6 and 7:

[Kings is a book in the Bible]

There are 42 values of cubits. I noticed right away that $42 = 3 \times 14$. Fourteen being 2×7 makes it a special number. The factor of three is necessary to make the 3 subsets to solve the puzzle.

Divide the 42 values of cubits into 3 subsets according to the order in the text and sum.

Subset 1

60, 20, 30, 20, 10, 5, 6, 7, 5, 20, 40, 20, 20, 20

Sum = 283

Subset 2

10, 5, 5, 10, 10, 10, 100, 50, 30, 50, 30, 10, 18, 12

Sum = 350

Subset 3

5, 5, 4, 10, 5, 30, 10, 4, 4, 3, 1, 1.5, 1.5, 4

Sum = 88

Multiplying with Sower's parable numbers (100-60-30):

100 x 283 = 28,300

60 x 350 = 21,000

30 x 88 = 2,640

Sum of products = 51,940, factors of **70 x 7**

Thus a biblical 70 x 7 is released.

Solution 2 in 2Chronicles chapters 3 and 4:

Chronicles is a book of the Bible

There are 21 values of cubits. Notice 21 = 7 x 3, seven being a special number in the Bible.

Arrange the 21 values of cubits in ascending order. Here are the 21 values: 5, 5, 5, 5, 5, 5, 10, 10, 10, 20, 20, 20, 20, 20, 20, 20, 20, 30, 35, 60, 120.

Next take "the Even and the Odd" (Q 89:3). This is an algorithm I stumbled upon while discovering Sower's Sevens in this text from the 7th century CE (side-bar "7th Century"). One might assume that latter text mimics 2Chronicles. And I feel this tends to validate my efforts if the same algorithm appears in a different text and produces the same result of **70 x 70**, many hundreds of years afterwards. Not only is the name of Solomon in common, but the construction of number sets is based on the same principle in both books.

Define three subsets of one value each:

>The first even number is 10

>The first odd number is 35

>The next even number is 60

Multiplying with Sower's parable numbers (100-60-30):

100 x 10 = 1,000

60 x 35 = 2,100

30 x 60 = 1,800

Sum of products = 4,900, factors of **70 x 70**

This is very unusual and phenomenal as a good result can be a mere **70 x 7**.

India the root of all earth's history

India is the cradle of the human race not Africa as they teach at school. All roads lead to India not Rome. Sanskrit is the purest form of all languages of which English and other European languages came from.

The Mayans, Aztecs, Egyptians, Phoenicians, Aryans and Aboriginals all have roots from India.

In Hinduism Kali is the wife of Shiva.

Cali-fornia named after Kali.

Cali-phate [Islam] named after Kali

A temple to Kali is found in Mexico.

Kal Yisroel means : All Isreal

Kali is the bride of Shiva, all of Israel. Just as Uma is the nation and bride of Shiva.

Cah Law : Bride [Jewish]

Chali : place in Palestine

Callirhoe : City near Haran

Kundalini [Hindu Yogic state] is also the name of an Aztec God of agriculture.

Maya is the goddess consort of Shiva. The Mayans are named after this Consort.

The sphinx in Egypt is Simha – the man lion a re-incarnation of the god Vishnu.

In Egypt : Seb, Geb, Sheba[f],Shibah[m] are all names for Shiva

The columns in Egypt are called matsSEBAH in Hebrew. A natsab is also a pillar.

Sebah = Shiva

Names like Bela, Asher, Issa, Baal, Jehovah, Sabbath, Moses, Mecca, Mohammed, Judah are all old SANSKRIT Gods.

You have Jews attending Ye-Shiva University in Israel to learn about Judaism.

The ritual for the dead is called Shiva in Jewish.

Seven / Shiva. In the black cube Muslim walk around you find a silver lingam [Vagina] it contains a meteorite broken into 7 pieces. 7 is the number of Shiva.

Shiva is the land of the seven.

Shaboth means to desist from exertion. This is Shabbath[Hebrew] = sabbath = Saba, Seba, Sheba, Tsaba = Shiva[Sanskrit]

Shiva means destroyer and in the bible then God as the destroyer passed over the land of Egypt.

Shiva is the lord of Yoga. Shiva means 7. Our body has 7 chakras.

Kannan = Kana.

In Tamil Hindu Kannan is the name of the promised land to pre Braham Vedic Hindu's.

It was symbolised by milk and honey.

Those who fled flood in India migrated to the Levant then on to Phoenicia etc

Brahma and Saraswati: like Abraham and Sarah. Both were brothers and sisters. The names are almost identical!

Brahma came from the land of the Oude.

Indians came from land of hodu.

India / Hoduw

Ex – Hodus / Exodus

Hodowi = Ho'doo = Hodu = Hindustan = India

Yehuwd = Yeh hood = Judah = Jewry = Judea

Yehud = Yehood, Jehud = place in Palistine

Yehudi = Yeh-hoo-dee = a Jew

In Sanskrit a hermitage is called a Vatica. In Rome we have the Vatican that was built on an old Vedic temple. Rome comes from Rama a Hindu God.

St Pauls, Dome on the rock are captured Vedic temples.

Allah means lord of 7 heavens just like Shiva. Bible says there are 7 heavens.

Krishna means anointed and is the same word Christ. See my book on Christ being a sacred secretion within us all.

Ishaak[Hebrew] = Isakhu[Sanskrit] means a friend of Shiva

Ishmael = Ish – Mahal = Great Shiva

Hara is root of Haran. [Home of Abraham]

Har means hill the preferred habitat of Shiva.

Hara is also the ancient city of Harappa – home to the devotees of Shiva

Pappah[Sanskrit] = pope

The Vatican was built on a Vedic hermitage.

There are no new religions just the old Indian religions recycled.

NUMBERS CONTINUED

THE 369 [KEY TO THE UNIVERSE –TESLA]

The representation of all master numbers connects to the universal sequence of 369.

0 – Tree of life, zero point

3 – Density line, creation for all. 3d. Creation, the triangle, the student, the third solution, the creation of a double charge, the progression through life.

6 – Perfect balance, which ideally transmit the will of God on earth. Heaven uniting with earth. Double-builder 33, the power of the material world, balance

9 – Completion, whole creation, all thought; divine, full circle, bio-energy, complete creation, power, brilliance, triple connection and balance.

Zero

Zero is a powerful number which brings great transformational change, sometimes occurring in a profound manner. It has much intensity, so caution is needed wherever it appears to ensure that extremes are not encountered.

Zero represents the Cosmic Egg, the primordial Androgyne – the Plenum. Zero as an empty circle depicts both the nothingness of death and yet the totality of life contained within the circle. As an ellipse the two sides represent ascent and descent, evolution and involution.

Before the One (meaning the Source—not the number) there is only Void, or non-being; thought; the ultimate mystery, the incomprehensible Absolute. Begins with meanings such

93

as, Non-existence; nothingness; the unmanifest; the unlimited; the eternal. The absence of all quality or quantity.

Taoism: It symbolizes the Void; non-being.

Buddhism: It is the Void and no-thingness.

Kabbalism: Boundless; Limitless Light; the Ain.

Pythagoras saw zero as the perfect. Zero is the Monad, the originator and container of All.

Islamic: Zero is the Divine Essence.

ONE   UNO

One: a number, numeral, and the name of the glyph representing that number. It is the natural number following 0 and preceding 2. It represents a single entity. One is sometimes referred to as unity or unit as an adjective. For example, a line segment of "unit length" is a line segment of length 1.

Is considered to be primordial unity: - The beginning and also the Creator. It the First Cause or as some cultures refer, the First Mover. One is the sum of all possibilities. It is essence, the Centre. One is referred to isolation. One springs forth, upsurges. It is seen as the number that gives cause to duality as multiplicity and back to final unity.

Chinese: refer to one as Yang, masculine; celestial. It is seen as an auspicious number. One is The Monad. Christian: God the Father; the Godhead.

Hebrew: Adonai, the Lord, the Most High, the "I AM", hidden intelligence.

Islamic: One refers to one as God as unity; the Absolute; self sufficient.

Pythagorean: One as meaning Spirit; God, from which all things come. It is the very essence, the Monad.

Taoism "Tao begets One, One begets Two, Two begets Three and three begets all things."

TWO   DUO

Duality. Alteration; diversity; conflict; dependence. Two is a static condition. It is rooted, seen as balance (two sides); stability; reflection. Two are the opposite poles. Represents the dual nature of the human being. It is desire, since all that is manifest in duality is in pairs of opposites. As One represents a point, two represents a length. The Binary is the first number to recede from Unity, it also symbolizes sin which deviates from the first good and denotes the transitory and the corruptible. Two represents two-fold strength—that is symbolized by two of anything, usually in history, by animals in pairs.

Cultural References

In Alchemy, two are the opposites, sun and moon. King and Queen. Sulphur and quicksilver, at first antagonistic but finally resolved and united in the Androgyne.

Buddhist: see two as the duality of samsara; male and female. Two is theory and practice; wisdom and method. It is blind and the lame united to see the way and to walk it.

Chinese, two is Yin, feminine; terrestrial; inauspicious.

Christian: Christ with two natures as God and human.

Revelation: Two is the number of witness. The disciples were sent out by two's (Mark 6:7). Two witnesses are required to establish truth (Deu 17:6, John 8:17, 2 Cor 13:1). Examples in Revelation are the beast out of the earth that has two horns like a lamb but spoke like a dragon (13:11). He is the false prophet. However the two witnesses are the true prophets of God (11:3).

Hebrew: Two is the life-force. In Qabalism wisdom and self-consciousness.

Hindu: Two is duality, the shakta-shakti.

Islamic: Two Spirit.

Platonic: Plato says two is a digit without meaning as it implies relationship, which introduces the third factor.

Pythagorean: Two is The Duad, the divided terrestrial being.

Taoist says two is representative of the K'ua, the Two. Two is a weak yin number as it has no centre.

The number 3.

The third dimension – we do things in threes so they will manifest in our physical realm.

Its roots stem from the meaning of multiplicity. Creative power; growth. Three is a moving forward of energy, overcoming duality, expression, manifestation and synthesis. Three is the first number to which the meaning "all" was given. It is The Triad, being the number of the whole as it contains the beginning, middle and an end.

The power of three is universal and is the tripartite nature of the world as heaven, earth, and waters. It is human as body, soul and spirit. Notice the distinction that soul and spirit are not the same. They are not. Three is birth, life, death. It is the beginning, middle and end. Three is a complete cycle unto itself. It is past, present, and the future.

The symbol of three is the triangle. Three interwoven circles or triangles can represent the indissoluble unity of the three persons of the trinity. Others symbols using three are: trident, fleur-de-lis, trefoil, trisula, thunderbolt, and trigrams.

The astral or emotional body stays connected to the physically body for three days after death. There is scientific evidence that the brain, even when all other systems are failing takes three days to register complete shutdown.

There are 3 phases to the moon. Lunar animals are often depicted as 3 legged.

Three is the heavenly number, representing soul, as four represents body. Together the two equal seven (3+4=7) and form the sacred hebdomad. The 3×4=12 representing the signs of the Zodiac and months of the year.

Pythagorean three means completion.

The symbol above, called a Triquetra (tri-KET a Latin word meaning 'three cornered')

Many believe the Triquetra is an ancient symbol of the female trinity, because it is composed of three interlaced yonic Vesica Pisces (a.k.a. Piscis is Latin for "Vessel of the Fish") and is the most basic and important construction in Sacred Geometry, which is the architecture of the universe.

A Vesica is formed when the circumference of two identical circles each pass through the centre of the other in effect creating a portal. 'The Triquetra' represents the 'Power of Three' or the threefold nature of existence i.e. body, mind and spirit; life, death and rebirth; past, present and future; beginning, middle and end; Sun, Moon and Earth; and the threefold co-creative process described as thought, word, and deed.

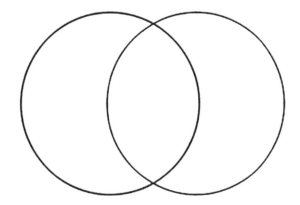

Sphere=ovum; with the vesica pisces in the middle

The creation process as described in the Vedas is unfolding, maintaining, and concluding as in birth, life and death. There are innumerable trinities and triads throughout myth and religious traditions, such as the triple goddess; maiden, mother, crone. One example in Greek mythology is Kore, Demeter, Hecate. The Christian trinity is Father, Son and Holy Ghost. Vedic trinities include Brahma, Vishnu and Shiva with their consorts Saraswati, Lakshmi and Kali to name just a few.

FOUR

Four is the 4th dimension = time which is illusion.
Four is seen as the first solid number. Spatial in scheme or in order of manifestation.
Static as opposed to the circular and the dynamic
Wholeness; totality; completion; solid
Earth; order
Rational – relativity and justice
Symbol of measurement
Foundation

There are four cardinal points; four seasons; four winds; four directions (as in North, South, East and West); four elements (Fire, Water, Air, Earth) in the western culture.

There are four sides to a square; four arms to a cross. There are four rivers to Paradise that formed a cross (the Garden of Eden was said to be within the four rivers). Within Paradise were four infernal regions, seas, and sacred mountains. There are four watches of the night and day, quarters of the moon. There are four quarters to the earth. There are four tetramorphs. The Divine Quaternity is in direct contrast to the Trinity. Four is a symbolic number used throughout in the Old Testament. The quaternary can be depicted as the quatrefoil as well as the square and the cross.

SIX

Six represents equilibrium; harmony – balance. It is the perfect number within the decad: 1+2+3=6. It is the most productive of all numbers.

It symbolizes union of polarity, the hermaphrodite being represented by the two interlaced triangles, the upward-pointing as male, fire and the heavens, and the downward-pointing as female, the waters and the earth.

Six is the symbol of luck; love; health; beauty; chance. It is a winning number at the throw of the dice in the West.

There are six rays of the solar wheel and there are six interlaced triangles. There are six pointed stars or Seal of Solomon – and Star of David – Merkabah

Chinese: Six represents Universe, with its four cardinal points and the above and below – making it a total of six directions. Chinese cultures there are six senses: taste, touch, smell, sight, and hearing, the sixth being mind. The day and night each have six periods.

Christian: Six is perfection; completion because man was created on the sixth day. Six is man's number. The most obvious use of this number is in the notorious passage containing 666.

(Rev 13:18 NIV) This calls for wisdom. If anyone has insight, let him calculate the number of the beast, for it is man's number. His number is 666.

Hebrew: There are six days of creation. It symbolizes meditation and intelligence.

Kabbalism: Six is creation, and beauty.

SEVEN

If 6 represents humanity then 7 – the centre of the spiral is humanity's connection to its source, god, the Christ consciousness [see my book Christ is within all] – or whatever name you prefer.

Seven is the number of the Universe. It is the three of the heavens (soul) combined with the four (body) of the earth; being the first number containing both the spiritual and the temporal. In looking over the list of meanings it doesn't take long to figure out why the seven has become significant in metaphysical, religious and other spiritual doctrines – as

101

seven represents the virginity of the Great Mother –
feminine archetype – She who creates.

There are 7
ages of man
ancient wonders of the world
circles of Universe
cosmic stages
days of the week
heavens
hells
pillars of wisdom
rays of the sun
musical notes – sound as frequency plays a key role in
matters of Universe. There are over 80 octaves of frequency
– each governing a specific manifestation in Universe.

In all cultures, myths and legends seven represents:-

Completeness and totality
macrocosm
perfection
plenty
reintegration
rest
security
safety
synthesis

The writings about the seven-headed dragon appear
throughout India, Persia, and the Far East, especially
Cambodia, but also Celtic and other Mediterranean myths.

The seventh ray of the sun is the path by which the human beings pass from this world to the next. Seven days is the period for fasting and penitence. The seventh power of any number, both square and a cube and thus was given great importance.

Alchemy – There are seven metals involved with the Work.

Astrology: There are seven stars of the Great Bear which are indestructible. There are seven Pleiades— sometimes referred to as the, Seven Sisters.

Buddhist: Seven is the number of ascent and of ascending to the highest; attaining the centre. The seven steps of Buddha symbolize the ascent of the seven cosmic stages transcending time and space. The seven-storied prasada at Borobudur is a sacred mountain and axis mundi, culminating in the transcendent North, reaching the realm of Buddha.

Nine is composed of the all-powerful 3×3.

It is the Triple Triad – Completion; fulfilment; attainment; beginning and the end; the whole number; a celestial and angelic number – the Earthly Paradise.

It is the number of the circumference, its division into 90 degrees and into 360 for the entire circumference.

Nine is symbolized by the two triangles which are a symbol of male, fire, mountain and female, water, and cave principles.

Buddhist tradition holds nine to be the supreme spiritual power and a celestial number.

10 = 1 = Rebirth – that which stirs and awakens your soul at this time.

Ten is the number of the cosmos—-the paradigm of creation. The decad contains all numbers and therefore all things and possibilities. It is the radix or turning point of all counting.

Ten is all-inclusive representing law; order and dominion. The tetraktys 1+2+3+4= 10 symbolizes divinity and one represents a point; two, length; three, a plane or surface (as a triangle); four, solidity or space.

It is seen as the perfect—the return to unity. When based on the digits of the two hands, it is completeness and the foundation of all counting. Its highest ranges of completeness, 100 and 1000, are the basis of all Hindu cosmology and in China the Ten Thousand Things, i.e.: the uncountable, symbolize the whole of manifestation.

Ten is also the number of completion of journeys and returns to origins: Odysseus wandered for nine years and returned on the tenth. Troy was besieged for nine years and fell on the tenth. Ten is the sum of the number nine of the circumference with the one of the centre—-being perfection. We see ten also being symbolized in rituals like the ritual of the Maypole – the one of the axis with the circle danced around.

Chinese: Represented by a cross formed centrally by the character chi, symbolizing the self facing both ways as both Yin and Yang, which is considered to be the perfect figure. The Ten Celestial Stems (Kan) are possibly connected with the names of the ten-day week on the prevailing cyclic calculations, as evident in the number sixty.

Christian: There are Ten Commandments of the Decalogue; as there are ten parables of the ten lamps, virgins, and talents. Tithes were to be given to God.

Gnostic: the ten Aeons become Sephiroth, emanating from the Pleroma.

number	NUMBERS in SQUARE	NUMBER TOTAL		SUM OF DIGITS	
2	4	10	1	1	
3	9	45	9	9	
4	16	136	10	1	
5	25	325	10	1	
6	36	666	18	9	
7	49	1225	10	1	
8	64	2080	10	1	
9	81	3321	9	9	
10	100	5050	10	1	
11	121	7381	19	10	1
12	144	10440	9	9	9
13	169	14365	19	10	1
14	196	19306	19	10	1
15	225	25425	18	9	9
16	256	32896	28	10	1
17	289	41905	19	10	1
18	324	52650	18	9	9
19	361	65341	19	10	1
20	400	80200	10	1	1
21	441	97461	27	9	

Magic squares summation

If we look at my excel spreadsheet I have started with the number 2. Thus a 2 x 2 magic square will have 4 numbers 1,2,3 and 4. They add up to 2 x 5 = 10.

Then by adding 1+0 in the result, I get 1 ; where these result is not a single digit I keep adding until I get the single digit result.

You can see you end up with the sequence 119119119.

We can also see that all trinity numbers like 111, 222 always give 9. A circle will add up to 9 (3+6+0). All Platonic shapes always add to 9.

In the Bible it says perfect year was 360 days. We now originally we only had 10 months. Julius Caesar and Augustus had months named after them. Yet October was the 8th month and December the 10th month. June is the 6th month. A 6 X 6 magic square contains 36 numbers this is a tenth of 360. A 6 x 6 magic square adds to 666 and numbers on perimeter add to number of days Noah on Ark. The magic square sequence is broken on the 18th and 19th – yet the Sun does change its cycles on the 18th. Each row on magic square adds to 111. Thus if you add cross to 666 you get 888 which is number Christ is in Gematria.

Etymology[THE ROOT OF OUR WORDS]

Understanding the root meaning of words and their significance.

"Signs and Symbols rule our world not words".

Just like our DNA is coded and Universe coded with mathematics. Our language is also coded and gives many clues to our divinity. The Bible is a cloak and under this cloak is hidden numerology, Gematria and a lot of wisdom. The Elites never wanted to share this hidden knowledge with normal people.

PERSPECTIVE

Per – speck – tive .

We are given a speck of the absolute. All drops in the ocean are pulled towards the ocean. Everyone is an individual note so who is the composer?

It is a state of nothing yet everything. How can anything begin that has no end? There is nothing to do as everything has already been done!

QUESTION

Quest is the act of Searching.

Ion means "to go".

Question thus means to go searching for something!

How does anything end where it begins? There is nowhere to go!

God is nowhere but now-here because God is also everywhere [Omnipotent].

There is no time to chase as God is every when. No need for power as power is retained. God sees everything as there is nothing to see! God controls everything as nothing to control.

God is alone as everything is one.

What is forever? That concept can't be fathomed. The All is unknowable. How can you measure the measureless?

If eternal life? How can it have a starting point? All beginnings are demarcated by their endings.

If an individual will exist eternally then eternity has already begun at conception.

So where does this lead us to? Answer it leads us to nowhere which is everywhere!

You can't wait for eternity as eternity would be outside of you. This makes eternity redundant. Eternity (absoluteness) by definition needs to envelop all things in all ways and by definition is unlimited.

If it has limits it is not absolute and therefore not of God.

God saves all or nothing. God does not work in divisions this is individualistic from Human ego and pseudo religions that control mans thoughts saying only our tribe will be saved.

SCRIBE

To scribe something (de-scribe) is to mark the outline of the thing. As soon as you do this you destroy the absolute totality. You can't give a name or definition to God without destroying what it really is. The all is unknowable.

To divide God is to destroy God. There are no outside saviours. [See my book Christ is within all]. Christ means oil it is a sacred secretion within every human being.

To create Heavens and Hells is to create boundaries and is false understanding. Again created by man not the creator.

PACE

'PACE' is found within the word Space.

Pace is the rate of vibration. The Universe is frequency, energy and Vibration.

Notes of music have to be played faster to occupy the same space but then have a shorter life span.

Too many notes lead to a cluttering or an offense. This can be likened to a trespass. There is only so much room between 'bars' (measures) or suns.

BAR

The Hebrew word 'bar' means son with phonetic interplay between the words son / sun. This gives us a hint to the musicality of the universe. We are all singing with one voice. If measures become too full then the volume increases. Volume is the magnitude of sound and the s'pace' that can be occupied in a 3D object.

911

9 x 11 = 99 percent capacity. A full bin / measure. Or Bin Laden

BIN

'BIN' from the Latin 'bini' means two by two.

Old English 'twinn' for twofold – ergo – twin towers.

9/11 is the energising call to the Phoenix to create a brand new age. [See my book on Satanists Rule over Us].

If volume is too loud the electric signals clip and thus distort.

DISTORT

'dis' = Pluto = apart /asunder.

Torsion = twisted like our DNA

French dix mean 10 = X

We have 40 weeks in Gestation [Number 40 mentioned a lot in the bible]

The French word 'quarante' is derived from the Latin 'quadraginta' this is akin to 'quattuor'.

The word means 4.

And 'quinta' the instrasitive verb means 20.

XL = 40 = chromosome pair that produces females

XX = 20 = chromosome pair that produces males.

Females have only X chromosomes and the male carries both X and Y. A single sperm will have either an X or a Y present.

Quarantine means 40 days.

108

108 x 20 = 2160 = [9]

2160 is the diameter of the moon

Uri Gagarin was in space for 108 minutes =[9]

10080 minutes in a week. =[9]

Five = phive = golden ratio of 0.618

MER

Mer means sea and is derived from Mere meaning Mother.

Mother = mater in Latin

Matter

From Middle English mater, matere, from Anglo-Norman matere, materie, from Old French materie, matiere, from Latin materia ("matter, stuff, material"), derivative of Latin mater ("mother"). Displaced native Middle English andweorc, andwork ("material, matter") (from Old English andweorc ("matter, substance, material")), Old English intinga ("matter, affair, business").

Maths is the measurement of all that matters.

Mother is an anagram of Thermo.

Anything from a mother needs heat to be incubated.

Mare means horse or dark side of moon.

Metric = matrix = admission into school.

Old English 'mæð' meant measure.

Maths is all done for the Mother.

INCUBATE

To bate means to beat. Every decade we decay with every beat of the hand of time. [Chronos].

LISTEN

Listen is an anagram of the word Silent.

113

How can you ever be silent and meditate if you are caught in the materialistic trap of all trying to compete and be the top dog?

Silence is the order of the Matrix within the mother. To be Mum [Mummy] means to be silent.

God put silence into the matrix of the mother. Many won't understand the significance of the number 40 in the Bible – it is the human gestation period!

Something Alien was introduced this had the ability to change mans physical / mental / emotional and spiritual states. Something that has been divided from its natural state would want to be saved. It was a transfer of sale.

Make the changed entity the property of someone else through transfer of sale. This has links to the world of commerce. If you feel divided you want to buy back your salvation.

Denominations are both religious and commercial. Credit is known as faith. Both Salvation and Salary are derived from SALT.

Pay means peace from the Latin word Pax. Christ was known as the Prince of Peace.

Sin is defined as debt. Sold is linked phonetically with Souled.

As one lives, one dies and then another lies. It is like deposits and withdrawals in a bank – the great endless cycle being played out.

The number 40 is the number associated with creating a new life.

The moon / woman's egg is the Davit boat that provides salvation for those lost at sea. The seamen. [Semen].

32 degrees on the mercury thermometer is 0 degrees centigrade of freezing. 33 degrees Fahrenheit is OFF – ICE thus death back into life. Cold is associated with darkness. The birth of a year and the death of a year. The word 'berth' means office.

MERCURY

Mercury = Marcari = Mecredi = Merci.

Means to trade or to buy.

French Merci = thank you for paying.

Mecredi is Wednesday in France.

Wednesday also means Wodan / Wotan. Wotan was shown tied to a tree.

Hermes also means a pile of stones in Greek, Thoth [Hermes] was the Pyramid builder. He is known as Enoch in the Bible.

Hermes / Mercury / Wodan. The wooden cross is symbolic of our DNA the cross we are nailed to.

Mer means to die also name Egyptians gave to their plough and Holy Woman.

Cury means to cure and is linked to the words curry and courier [speed]. Mercury was also called quicksilver and the messenger of the Gods.

SEN-TENCE

Tense = 10 = X

X MEANS WRONG TO CROSS OUT

The word check point to a King this is what cashing a check implies.

Once you purchase in a shop you go to the EXIT where you are crossed out – you no longer matter. Cashiers also called tellers. It is the Human Desire for Personal advantage that keep the commercial world flowing.

Humans want to conquer anyone who does not serve their own personal selfish purpose. A selfish person may lose all his friends then change his habits but he is still being selfish – he is still thinking about only his self and his poor ego.

The simple truth is true religion needs to be found not from human pseudo religious ideas created for control.

Religion means the bringing together of man and god in union.

116

True salvation comes only from within and not by going to the church or the temple or the Mosque.

Individuals create a template for their own destruction and are never satisfied with their lot in life or where one is. ION comes from where one is and is linked to the Egyptian Goddess Isis.

God at source is just a single Monad. No matter where God is there God Is!

The dualistic nature of reality we perceive to be true. The black / white and the Good / Evil are not the original.

Anything with a being inside within the ages will age. God is outside and yet within.

Time moves in a circular fashion. Einstein knew that past, present and future time could all exist at the same time depending on the observer's position in space.

The Gods of Genesis called the Elohim [plural for Gods] kept men silent by using the secrets of sine waves being out of phase. It is good versus evil due to man's love of competition always trying to compete for the best food and females.

All advancements have already been made on the last time the wheel of time went round. [See my book on Age of Aquarius]

Washington DC and the USA

If we look at the symbol on the American dollar it is an unfinished pyramid with an all seeing eye at the top.

If we overlay this pattern over the grid pattern over the grid system in Washington D.C and poke a hole throw the eye then it leads us to House of the Temple – the Scottish Freemasons temple in Washington. This is modelled on the temple of King Mausolus where we get the world Mausoleum from. Albert Pike 33 Mason is buried in the building. The building has 33 columns and is 33 feet high.

Number 33

Jesus did 33 miracles and died at age 33.

Human body has 33 vertebrae.

[See my book Christ is within all]

We have Runway 33 at Cape Canaveral. NASA

King David ruled 33 years.

True knowledge of the 33 comes from understanding that Christ means oil and is a sacred secretion within all [See my book on Amazon]

10 Sephiroth on the tree of life that is found on the flower of life.

1 hidden Sephiroth DA'ATH [often not shown]

22 paths = 33

Middle C is 33 harmonics. 261.6Hz 4 C key on 88 key piano.

32 overtones above Schumann resonance frequency of Earth. 7.83Hz

Overtone has a broader meaning: "any higher frequency above the fundamental which is simultaneously produced."

261.6 / 7.83 = 33.4

The UN emblem divides the world into 33 sectors.

Great seal of USA – Left wing 33 feathers, Right wing =32 and tail =9

Two vesica piscis on dollar create the Star of David, Solomon's seal, symbol of the Rothschild's. These points to the letters MASON when re-arranged.

In Washington D.C we find Rosslyn Virginia just like we find Rosslyn chapel in Scotland built by the Knights Templars who then became the Freemasons after being wiped out by the King of France and fleeing to Scotland.

We can trace a path above the all Seeing Eye in Washington DC it leads to the Marines Memorial.

A Royal mile is 8/7 of a normal mile. This is the distance between Holyrood and Edinburgh castle. The main street in Edinburgh is called the Royal mile and leads to the castle.

Thus the Royal mile is the Egyptian Royal mile.

Did the King of Scotland who built Holyrood learn these secret measurements from the escaping Templars?

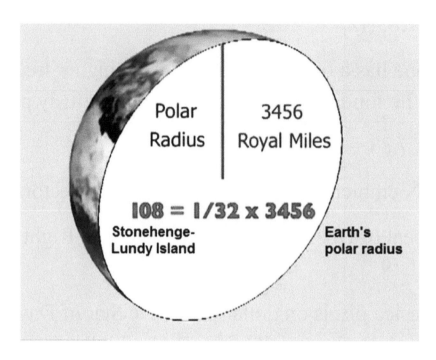

Polar Radius | 3456 Royal Miles

108 = 1/32 x 3456
Stonehenge-Lundy Island

Earth's polar radius

3456 Royal miles is the polar radius of our earth.

Washington D.C

All major nodes like the White House and Jefferson building are 1 Royal mile apart in Washington DC. It is built around a large cube pattern and Masonic compasses can be found within this pattern.

1728 x 2 royal miles = 3456

This links the cube found in Washington DC to the book of Revelations within the bible. The cube has a volume of 1728 furlongs – see Revelation 21:16 where it describes the New Jerusalem. No wonder the USA favours Israel.

A tree of life called Portaelucis *[1516] matches the Washington DC architecture. [* this means portal of life].

We find Scotts circle = DA'aath in Washington DC it is the letter Y representing the choice between doing good or bad!

The flower of life is 6 circles around an inner one. The tree of life is found on this. If we extend we get 13 circles as all trees bear fruit. Connecting these 13 circles we get Metatrons Cube [Enoch] which contains all the 5 platonic solids within the central cube just like fractals.

Tetractys

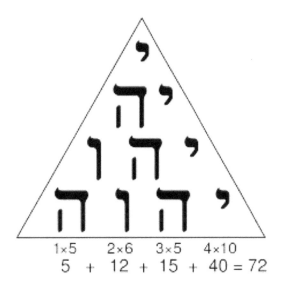

The Tetractys above is the triangle of Enoch it encodes the name of God from the Tetragrammaton to 72.

Enoch died at 365 years old another solar reference.

121

The USA dollar has a Tetractys – 13 stars above the Eagles head. We have 13 stripes on the shield, 13 colonies.

These 13 stars on the Yankee dollar represent the junctions found within Metatron's cube.

We have 72 arrangements of the 4 holy letters of the tetragrammatron. Every 72 years the zodiac moves by 1 degree.

Pennsylvania Avenue is aligned with the star Sirius.

The federal triangle {zodiac} link Washington DC to Virgo [Isis]

Isis, Virgo over Federal Triangle and Osiris, Leo over the Capital building.

The Washington Monument is the penis of Osiris held in its hand by Virgo [Isis]

The number for Isis is 7, we also have the 7 Rays. Apollo also had 7 points on his head as did the Colossus of Rhodes, The Statue of Liberty too has 7 points.

The Washington monument is 6,660 inches high or 555 feet.

This then projects the Octagram onto the ground.

This in Sumeria was called the Star of Inanna.

Sumeria only discovered 1890 thus most references call it the Star of Isis.

The Octagram star is a male solar symbol. It can be found it the Celtic calendar, Gnostics, Rub el Hizb, and even the Aztec calendar. The eight pointed star is a Gnostic symbol, known as the "Octagram of Creation." It is associated with Venus, and is also sacred to Ishtar [Easter] Eostre Anglo-Saxon Goddess of fertility.

We have a stretched Vesica Pisces at the Washington Monument. The Great Pyramid of Egypt fits into this Vulva. Both have phi the Golden ratio in their mathematics.

DC > Central Park > Stonehenge dissects Central Park into triangles. The aqueduct in Central Park dissects this line. An Octagon surrounds Cleopatra's needle in Central Park. This is a twin obelisk with the other being in London. Originally they stood outside the Temple of Heliopolis [Where Saturn our first sun was worshipped].

The aqueduct points to the Temple of Dendur this Egyptian Temple was moved to the USA when the Aswan dam was being built.

The statue of Liberty which has 7 points in her head, the corner stone was laid in a Masonic ceremony. Masons paid a fortune to move obelisks around the world.

Isis is the Goddess of the Sun just like Apollo to the Greeks.

Statue of Liberty is 111 feet and 1 inch high = Isis.

In Freemasonry Boaz the left column is the Sun and Joachim the right column is the moon. These are the Pineal and pituitary glands in our brains. Abraham is Pineal is sun, Sarah is pituitary is moon. Hence Ra-Ra.

We have a 5:12 ratio in triangle at Stonehenge and Washington D.C

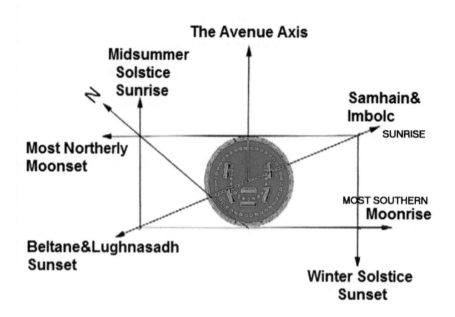

Stonehenge was built when Egypt was at its peak.

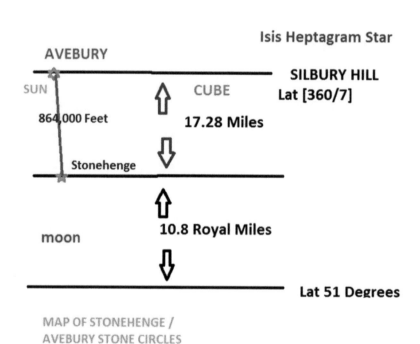

MAP OF STONEHENGE /
AVEBURY STONE CIRCLES

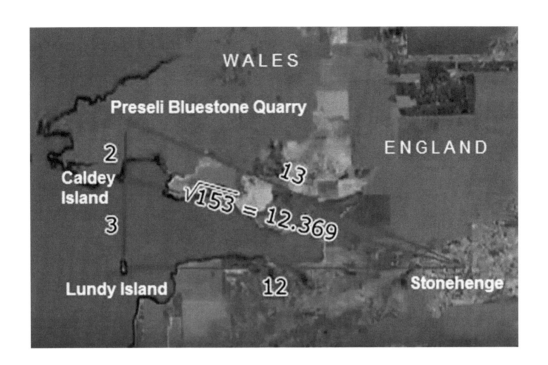

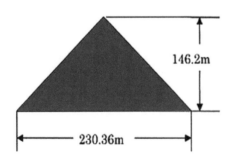

the volume of the great pyramid

2,586,069 m³   →   × 4/3 π   =   1.0832 × 10⁷m³

the volume of the Earth

4/3 π × (equator radius)² × (polar radius)   =   1.0832 × 10²¹m³

127

We can see that the Pyramid is a scaled down model of the Earth.

From the Map of Stonehenge I have shown they decoded the Moon, the Sun, the Cube and the Star of Isis into their design.

The great triangle made by the Stonehenge, Lundy and Presili points is 2500 larger than the triangle created by the 4 standing stones in the centre of Stonehenge. This is the great temple. Stonehenge being the middle temple.

Averbury to Stonehenge is 864,000 feet. Diameter of the Sun is 864,000. How could primitive people calculate the Earths diameter?

Stonehenge to Lundy is 123.4 miles

Statute mile is 5280 feet

123.4 miles = 108 Royal miles this is 1/32 of the radius of the Earth.

108 = 1/32 x 3456 : A number sacred in many religions they are worshipping the moon. 3456 is the Polar Radius.

Equator Circumference = 360,000 x 365.242

= number of days in a year x 360 [degrees in a circle] x 1000

12^5 / 10 miles = meridian circumference of the earth.

5280 feet in one mile.

528 Hz is a Solfeggio frequency

$\sqrt{153}$ = 12.369 is the number of full moons in a year

Isaac Newton [Alchemist] used scale 33 degrees temperature waters boils at and 0 degrees where it freezes. Again linking to the 33 where everything below 33 is not alive.

The pyramid is at 29.972 degree latitude North.

These are the same numbers as the speed of light

Speed of light is 299,792,458 metres / second.

The meter seems to be an old measurement re-born.

In the Jewish language Yod which looks like a dot or a comma has a numerical value of 10 in Gematria.

Yod represents the origin of all things.

Yod is used to create all other letters in the Hebrew alphabet. The Aleph looks like a N but is made up of 4 Yods opposite each other.

Yod is the Ego = 10

He = none Ego = 5 [passive]

Vau = Affinity between the Ego and the None Ego = 6 [10 =1 + 5)

Je-hov-vaH

Starts with J = 10 . 10 represents the something coming from nothing. Ends with H. H is the 8 letter on its side 8 represents infinity / eternity.

Tarot based on Rota , the wheel of the Zodiac

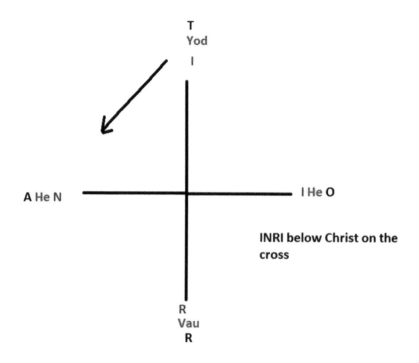

The human brain has 10^{11} neurons but also 10^{18} microtubules. This is the same number as age of the Universe in seconds.

I hope I have given something to muse over and to encourage you to do your own research. Stop wasting time playing video games and try and educate yourself.

The Number 22

What are the chances of the 8 attacks below spread out over 6 years and in 6 different countries would all be carried out on the 22nd of the month?
Norway attack 22-07-11
Lee Rigby 22-05-2013
Pakistan tourist shooting 22-06-13
Canada shootings parliament 22-10-14
Brussels attack 22-03-16
Munich attack 22-07-16
London Westminster attack 22-03-17
Manchester Arena attack 22-05-17

Manchester attack happened at 22:00, 22 died on the 22nd – done by a 22 years old Salman Abedi.
22nd is a significant number for Jews they blew up the King David Hotel British Headquarters on July 22nd 1946 and killed 91 civilians. The Jewish terrorists dressed up as Palestinian Arabs to plant their bombs.

Those trying to destroy ISIS are Russia and Syrian forces so why is ISIS not attacking Russia but Europe? It is the Hegelian dialect problem, reaction, solution. They create the problem then offer us the solution. The solution they wanted in the first place. The solution is war against Israel's enemies.

ISIS was created by Mossad to destabilise Iraq and Syria

and used as an excuse for terrorist atrocities in Britain, America and Europe.

Look at operation Northwood how America planned a false flag – an attack on an American city that would be blamed on Cuba – this then could be used to justify war with Cuba. If we look at the Sandy Hook shooting we see the same female crisis actor saying she was a classmate of the shooter Adam Lanza [Alexa Israel]. We see this same actress in another news item posing as the sister of James Foley. Many who say they are Al Qaeda spokesmen are Israeli actors. Adam Gadahn, Al Qaeda spokesperson, turns out to be a Jew called Adam Pearlman. Simon Elliot [Elliot Shimon] aka Al-Baghdadi was born to two Jewish parents and is a MOSSAD agent.

President John F. Kennedy was assassinated on November 22, 1963, in a public square which had been home to a Masonic Lodge and which has an obelisk in its centre. November is Month #11 and the day of the murder was the 22nd. Numbers 11 and 22 are sacred primary occult numbers.

Number 22
In numerology 22 is one of the most powerful of all numbers. It is often called the Master Builder. The 22 can turn the most ambitious of dreams into reality. It is potentially the most successful of all numbers. It has many of the inspirational insights of the 11, combined with the

practicality and methodical nature of the 4, its sum. JFK was assassinated on 11/22.

22 – The MASTER BUILDER

Number 22 is the number of the Spiritual Master Builder on the Material plane. 22 synthesizes and expands the powers of **11**. There is four times the power and energy in this vibration so there is four times the strength to use on the material plane. This is the 'God' energy brought to the material plane and put into form, and this vibration holds with it a great deal of responsibility. Because of its great power, the number 22 may result in outstanding ascendancy or disastrous downfall.

The Master Number 22 symbolizes the principle of precision and balance. When it senses its full capacity as a 'Master Builder', it can achieve what is hardly imaginable. The 22 can turn the most ambitious of dreams into reality and is potentially the most successful of all numbers.

Master Number 22 carries many of the inspirational insights of the **number 11**, combined with the practicality and methodical nature of the **4** energy. It is unlimited, yet disciplined. It sees the archetype and brings it down to earth in some material form.

133

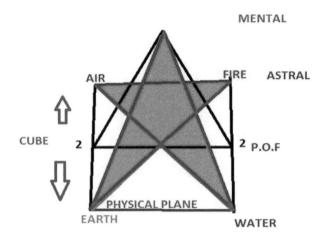

MENTAL

AIR · FIRE · ASTRAL

CUBE · 2 · 2 P.O.F

PHYSICAL PLANE

EARTH · WATER

22 CREATES THE CUBE
AND THE PENTAGON

Gematria and numerology

http://www.gematrinator.com/calculator/index.php

There is a Gematria calculator on the above link you can check my findings.

I am using the codes FR for Full reduction and RFR for Reverse Full Reduction

List of words with a value of 33

People [fr]   Person [fr]   Pineal [rfr]

Masonry [fr] Secrecy [fr] Order [fr]

Bible [fr] Believe [fr]

Amen [English Ordinal]

Genesis [fr]

List of words with a value of 58

Freemasonry [fr]

Kundalini [rfr]

Craftsman [rfr]

We the people [fr]

In god we trust [fr]

Annuit coeptis [fr]

Rosicrucian [fr]

Rose Cross [fr]

Decoding Osiris

The Blackstar is the Black Moon of Death.

December is the 10th month

Decay = end of the year = death.

December 25th birth of Mithras and other Gods as shortest day so Sun born again [Astro Theology]

December the 19th = 10 / 19 = 1+0 / 19 = 119 = 911 in reverse remember some languages like Jewish and Arabic are read right to left and are the origin of all languages.

Osiris = O Sirius = Black = Ausar = L Auzarus

Sirius = Osiris [Ausar] = Czar

Assyria [Ashur]

= Azura Mazda

The word Syrian's come from the Assyrians

OSIRIS, O Syria, Assyria, Syrius, Syrian

Ashur is the name of the Sun but also the name given to the Capital of Iraq.

SAR = Prince = TSAR / CZAR/ CEASAR

THE TRINITY OF GODS

BAAL HADAD, EL ASHUR[ASURA]. ANAT[ASHERAH] = Queen of Heaven.

Horus = Child

OSIRIS [AUSAR] = SUN = FATHER

ISIS = ESAT = EAST = Queen of Heaven

ORION is same name as OSIRIS in hieroglyphics

ISIS same as SIRIUS

SIRIUS / VENUS are both morning stars both very bright and rise before the Sun in the East. Morning Star = Lucifer = The Light bringer.

How Are Tesla's numbers 3,6 and 9 found in the Great Pyramid at Giza?

To quote Tesla he said that the numbers 3, 6 and 9 are the key to the universe. He also believed that there is so much electro-magnetic energy flowing around the earth that if this could be tapped into then he could have provided the earth with free wireless energy.

The Zodiac moves 1 degree for every 72 years when viewed from same place on Earth. 7+ 2 = 9

Base circumference of Pyramid = 43200

4+3+2+0+0 = 9

The pyramid is a scaled down model of the Northern hemisphere.

Divide 432000 / 72 = 600 = 6

Latitude of Pyramid = 30 degrees = 3+0 = 3

Full Zodiac Cycle is 25920 years = 9

Equinoxes

Very important to ancient people as they allowed the tracking of stars and planets in the sky to be noted. Many Esoteric thinkers believe it is the Zodiac Sign in the East when you are born that is the important one, not your birth sign.

Christ was around in the Age of Pisces which is the Fish, is this why Pope has a Fish mouth shaped hat?

1 degree = 72 years

We have 30 degrees per Zodiac Sign [1/12]

30 x 72 = 2160

Full Age = 2160 x 12 = 25920

[See my book Age of Aquarius for more on these Great Cycles]

The All Seeing Eye

The All Seeing Eye is a very old symbol that belongs to Nimrod. Nimrod built a Tower Of Babel to keep an eye on his people below. This All Seeing Eye Symbol was later adopted by societies like The Illuminati. The Tower of Babel was destroyed by God? The people were scattered and could no longer communicate to each other so did so using symbols. But what was the real purpose of this tower? In Mexico archaeologists found a large reservoir of mercury under a Pyramid they concluded that it was there just to represent a river into the underworld. Yet mercury is a superconductor and can be used for rocket fuel. Names in the Grand Canyon have Egyptian names. There seems to be links between the Pyramids in Mexico and Egypt [Did Thoth help create both?]. Yet science tells us South America and Africa split millions of years ago. What is the true age of the Pyramids? Ancient technology has been found on Earth far superior to what we have now. Does everything happen in cycles technology advancing until Earth destroys itself in a

Nuclear War? There is evidence of previous Nuclear Wars in India etc

Other Names for Nimrod

1. Marduk, from which comes Mars.

2. Enki, god of wisdom, incantations and deep waters of the oceans.

3. Apsu, from which comes Poseidon.

4. Astalluhi, god of healing and exorcism. In Greek, Aesculapeus.

5. Bel / Baal, means "lord" or "master".

6. Nabul / Nebo, known to Romans as Apollo, in Greek as Hermes.

The names Nabul and Bel were the official names of Nimrod/Marduk in later periods and were popular in later periods among the ruling classes of Babylon as name elements as in NEBUchadnezzar and BELshazzar.

Other Names for Tammuz

1. Osiris (Egyptian, mother (Semiramis) was known as Isis).

2. Adonis (mother was Venus)

3. Krishna (mother was Devaki)

4. Iswara (mother was Isi)

139

5. Deoius (mother was Cybele)

6. Platus (mother was Irene)

7. Jupiter (mother was Fortuna)

Tammuz was born during the winter solstice on December 25th. His birthday was celebrated throughout Babylonia and surrounding areas. Tammuz died in his 40th year while boar hunting in the spring. In honour of him, the people mourned his death each spring for 40 days, one day for each year of his life. After the forty-day fast, a joyful feast of Ishtar (Easter)[Oestre – Anglo-Saxon Goddess] took place. At this feast coloured eggs were exchanged and eaten as a symbol of the death and resurrection of Tammuz in the spring crops. A feast of ham, symbolizing victory over the boar that killed Tammuz, was enjoyed by all. Finally cakes marked with the letter "T" (to remind everyone of Tammuz) were baked and eaten (Hot cross buns).

That the worship of Nimrod and Semiramis is the origin of all the pagan systems on earth.

The number 40 is used a lot in the Bible it is simply the number of weeks a woman is pregnant for. Most miracles happen in the Bible on the certain day in the month of Nissan. The odds on this are billions to one. Yet this date is an equinox and the time when crops were harvested and feasts held.

Nimrod "began to become a [giant] mighty one" through some sort of defilement of himself. In the context of numerous other descriptions of this man, the word "gibbor" in this case was more than just a "mighty one" - Nimrod *became* a giant. Somehow, he activated Nephilim genes that apparently came to him through his ancestry. Thus, he became a Post-Flood member of the *Demi-god Tier* - an offspring of the Nephilim.

He built the Tower of Babel with intentions of killing God and taking over - a plan that was not at all unlike that of Zeus, the Olympian who sought to destroy the Titan gods who ruled before him. But Nimrod's plans were thwarted by God and the people of the earth who supported him were divided into 70 languages/nations. Each people group went away talking about the same guy, only now, he had other names. The dominant name he became known by was Osiris, the god of the Egyptians. Let's look a little deeper into this myth and how it played into the characters and events of our Hebrew Bible.

The Egyptian god family tree.

Atum [Atom, Adam] is the *Ultimate Source Tier* god. Shu and Tefnut are the *Top Tier* gods, followed by Geb and Nut in the *Middle Tier* and Osiris is in the *Final Tier* (the same tier that we found Dionysus, Apollo, Marduk, Ninurta and Gilgamesh - all of which are other names for Nimrod). Similar to Marduk in the Sumerian family tree, Osiris rises from the *Final Tier* to be the ultimate, ruling deity in Egyptian mythology.

Secrets of the Beehive

But one of the first things people notice about bees is that they are attracted to sweet things and not foul. There are about 30,000 species of bees. Our main concern is with one - the honeybee. So when I say bee, I mean honeybee.

In 1923, a scientist named von Frisch published his famous work on the dance of the bee. When a bee discovers a source of food, she fills herself with the nectar and returns to the hive. She then performs what has been termed a dance which symbolically describes where the food source is. From this symbolic ritual, the other bees can find the source.

Reproduction is interesting. Not all bees have two parents. We have three classes: the queen, the female workers, and the male drones. The one special fertile female is the queen. There are other females but they do not produce any eggs. The male bees are produced by the queen's unfertilized eggs (in other words - no father). The females are produced when the queen has mated with a male - therefore she has two parents.

Interestingly, the family tree of a colony produces what we know as the Fibonacci sequence. A bee's ancestry fits the exact pattern. Draw out the example.

Great- great, great gt, gt, gt

Grand- grand- grand grand

Number of parents: parents: parents: parents: parents:

Of a MALE bee: 1 2 3 5 8

Of a FEMALE bee: 2 3 5 8 13

0, 1, 1, 2, 3, 5, 8, 13, 21, 34, 55, 89, 144, 233, 377, 610, 987...

As you may or may not know, the Fibonacci sequence is one of the major chords played by Nature in her symphony. Everywhere one looks there is the sequence displayed: view the construction of sunflowers, pinecones, pineapples, artichokes, apples, lemons, starfish, sand dollars, the iris, buttercup, daisies, and you could go on and on.

It is the proportion of living things. One author gives this definition: "The Fibonacci sequence actually begins with two terms, zero and unity, nothing and everything, the Unknowable and the manifest Monad. These are the first two terms. Their sum, another unity, is the third term. To find each next term, just add the two latest terms together. This process produces the endless series 0,1,2,3,5,8,13,21,34,55,89,144 ... At first glance we see a chain of numbers. But look beyond the visible numbers to the self-accumulating process by which they grow. The series grows by accruing terms that come from within itself, from its immediate past, taking nothing from outside the sequence for its growth. Each term may be traced back to its beginning as unity in the Monad, which itself arose from the incomprehensible mystery of zero.

This principle of ongoing growth-from-within is the essence of the Pentad's principle of regeneration and the pulsing rhythms of natural growth and dissolution." (Michael Schneider, A Beginner's Guide to Constructing the Universe)

Other examples:

Fibonacci example: of Bee moving over a honeycomb. Let's see how these numbers relate one to the other.

Do hexagram example. Ask: how do you produce a hexagram? It is the relation of the radius to the circumference. To create the hexagram, draw a circle. Use the compass, keep the radius the same and place the point anywhere upon the circumference. Mark a small arc on the circle and then place the point on that arc and make another one. Continue all the way around the circle until you return to the beginning. There will be six points.

Thus is illustrated why the Point and Circle (as symbol of the Sun)is related to the hexagram and the number six.

Talk about relationship of the pentagram to the Fibonacci sequence. The Pentagram (growth and regeneration/golden proportions, golden rectangle, golden spiral)

Looking back to Egypt, bees were considered tears of the sun-god RA. Here we see a relationship with the sun that we will see later. The bee hieroglyphic is a symbol of Lower Egypt. Because of the sudden appearances of bees they became symbols of death and rebirth. Bees also represented the soul. Honey was often offered to deities.

In Hindu myth and iconography, the bee surmounting a triangle is a symbol of Shiva. Sometimes we see a blue bee on the forehead of Krishna, as the avatar of Vishnu. Kama, the god of love, like Cupid has a bow and arrows, and the bow string is made up of bees. In the yogic doctrine, where each chakra emits a different sound in meditation, the lowest chakra (muldhahara) emits a hum likened in the writings to a bumblebee. Note that the first chakra represents our strongest bond to the material world and Eros or Cupid in Greek philosophy is the natural impelling force towards sensual objects.

Further in the ancient Greek world, for the Orphics the bee symbolized the soul because they migrated in swarms. The second temple built at Delphi was said to be built by bees. The god of love, Cupid, is often pictured with bees or being stung. Here is a famous painting: SHOW PAINTING. In the myth it is written that Venus says to her son after he is stung: "Thou too art like a bee, for although a tiny child, yet how terrible are the wounds thou dost inflict!" Periclymenus, one of the Argonauts, was granted by Poseidon the power of changing his shape into a lion, a snake, or a bee. Throughout the Mediterranean the bee was also a symbol of spring because it was associated with the blooming gorse (a broom) that turned the hillsides all over the region bright yellow as soon as the Sun's light increased. As soon as this happened the bee appeared.

Here is another connection of the bee with the sun and with the idea of resurrection.

A fascinating connection regards the Rites of Eleusis. These mystery rites were widely regarded as the high point of Greek religion. They centered on the goddess Demeter who was the Great Mother deity. The myth regarded nature's seasonal death and resurrection and represented it in the story of Demeter, her daughter Persephone and her abduction by Hades. Persephone or Kore was sometimes called honey-like and the moon (among other reasons because the moon is also called a bull and Taurus is its exaltation). The rites were conducted by the Hierophant and Hiera, the Hierophantides (2 females) and the Panageis Priestesses or Milissae - meaning bees. The function of these priestesses is still not known.

There are coins from Ephesus from the 5th century B.C. that depict a queen bee as a symbol of the Great Mother. Ephesus was known throughout the ancient world for its temple to the Great Mother Goddess.

In the Roman Mithraic rites, there were different levels or grades of initiation. One was termed the Degree of the Lion. The neoplatonic philosopher Porphyry writes: "The theologians have used honey to symbolize many different things since it combines multiple powers, and is both cathartic and preservative in its effects. Many things are kept from rotting by honey and it clears up persistent wounds. It is sweet to the taste and is gathered from flowers by bees which incidentally are born from cattle.

When they pour honey instead of water on the initiates in the Lion Mysteries, they call upon them to keep their hands pure of all that which is painful, harmful, or dirty ..."

(Porphyry, On the Cave of the Nymphs) Porphyry also says that souls coming into the world are "born from cattle, and the god who secretly impedes incarnation is "the cattle thief".

What could he mean by this statement - born from cattle? It seems that Porphyry is making an allusion to the Neoplatonic principle that souls descend into incarnation (the Many) and ascend back to the Monad (the One). The summer and winter solstice being the two gates (sometimes referred to as "mouths") in this process: the gate of Cancer (summer solstice) being the one through which souls descend and the gate of Capricorn (winter solstice) being the one for ascending. The key to Porphyry's statement is hidden in the astrological symbols. The sign of Cancer is ruled by the moon (Kore was sometimes called the moon and also Melitodes meaning "honey-like") Souls were thought to descend into incarnation from the lunar sphere. And the moon is exalted in the sign of Taurus, the Bull. Recall the Taurus symbol: the crescent crowning the circle. Thus, souls are born from cattle.

If we can go back to Egypt quickly I want to point out that at Memphis, the Memphite theology, the Apis bull was worshipped as the ba (or spirit or spiritual manifestation) of Ptah, the creator of the universe. Ptah's symbols were the architect's transit, level, and plumb line. He was the patron of skilled craftsmen and architects.

The Number 7

THE NUMBER SEVEN AND OUR BODY

* Our body has seven parts, the head, chest, abdomen, two legs and two arms

* Our 7th body part that rules all else, is the head with the mind that has seven parts for external use, two eyes, two ears, two nostrils and a mouth.

* We have seven internal organs, stomach, liver, heart, lungs, spleen and two kidneys.

* An adult is made up of around 7,000,000,000,000,000,000,000,000,000 (7 octillion) atoms.

* The Seven DNA Polymerase Families that can be further subdivided into seven different families: A, B, C, D, X, Y, and RT.

* Seven endocrines glands in the human body

* Seven Senses or Chakras [see later for how these relate to the planets]

* The Seven bodies of the Human microcosm.

* Our voice is made in seven tones

* The Alchemists of the middle ages counted the following seven bodies: Sun- Gold, Moon- Silver, Mars- Iron,

Mercury- Quicksilver, Saturn- Lead, Jupiter- Tin, Venus-Copper.

IN THE HEAVENS

* 7 classical planets

* The Moon passes through stages of 7 days in increase, full, decrease, and renewal.

* 7 colours on the rainbow

* 7 days on a week

* 7 sisters on the Pleiades

7 of Revelation. IN THE BIBLE

* The Seven Seals

* The Seven Churches

* Seven years for Repentance;

* Seven churches of Asia (or Assiah)

* Seven Angels with Trumpets

* Seven candlesticks of the Holy Places

* Seven Spirits stand before the Throne of God: Michael, Gabriel, Lamael, Raphael, Zachariel, Anael, and Oriphel. (Gustavini.)

* Seven trumpets

* Seven lamp stands

* Seven stars

* Seven kings

* Seven thousands slain,

* Seven vials of wrath to be poured out, pace the Apocalypse

* Seven vices

* Seven dips in Jordan, to cleanse himself from Leprosy

* The seven spirits of God: 1. The Spirit of Wisdom. 2. The Spirit of Understanding. 3. The Spirit of Counsel. 4. The Spirit of Power. 5. The Spirit of Knowledge. 6. The Spirit of Righteousness. 7. The Spirit of Divine Awfulness.

* The seven deadly sins are: Pride, Wrath, Envy, Lust, Gluttony, Avarice and Sloth.

* The seven virtues are: Faith, Hope, Charity, Prudence, Justice, Fortitude and Temperance. The first three are called "the holy virtues." (See Seven Deadly Sins.)

* The seven joys of the Virgin Mary are: The Annunciation, Visitation, Nativity, Adoration of the Magi, Presentation in the Temple, Finding Christ amongst the Doctors, and the Assumption.

* The seven sorrows of the Virgin Mary are: Simeon's Prophecy, the Flight into Egypt, Christ Missed, the Betrayal, the Crucifixion, the Taking Down from the Cross, and the Ascension, when she was left alone.

* Whoever touches a human corpse will be unclean for seven days. – Numbers 19:11

* Jericho were encompassed seven days, by seven priests, bearing seven rams' horns

* Solomon was seven years building the Temple, which was dedicated in the seventh month

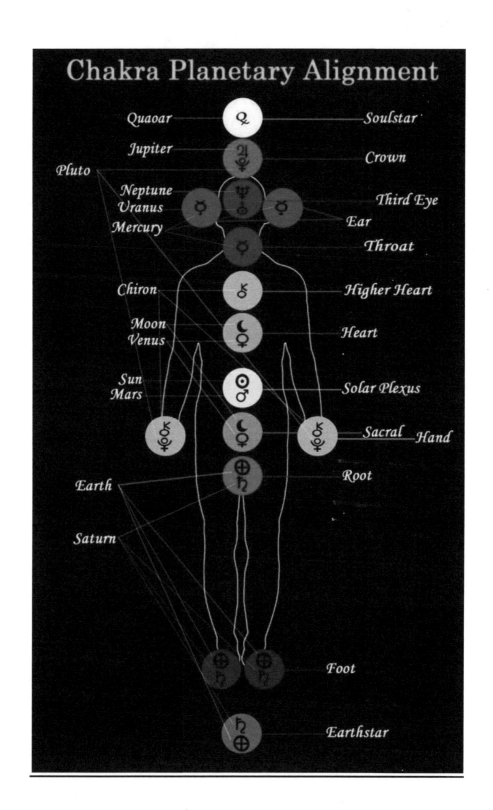

Chakra Planetary Alignment

152

I was exposing the New World Satanic Order. Amazon banned my books, Amazon are part of this Cabal.

My books are available still on Lulu, Barnes and Noble.

Unfortunately Amazon dominates the book market, especially e-books. So many of my ex readers won't know my books are still available. I have seen on E-bay someone trying to sell one second hand for £30.

adrianbonni@gmx.com

Please give feedback whether good or bad, or send me your questions.

86% OF CHILDREN SUFFERED AN ADVERSE REACTION TO THE PFIZER C19 VACCINE IN THE CLINICAL TRIAL

of 1,127 children who received a first dose of the jab, 86% experienced an adverse reaction.

of 1,097 children who received a 2nd dose of the jab, 78.9% experienced an adverse reaction.

https://web.archive.org/web/20230000000000*/https://www.fda.gov/media/144413/download